If A Passive-Progressive Leads from Behind, he is A Double Oxymoron

A COLLECTION OF SATIRE

"On the one hand, then again on the other . . ."

Don Storch

Copyright and publishers
Copyright © 2014 Don Storch
All rights reserved.

ISBN: 1500955639
ISBN 13: 9781500955632

DEDICATION

This book is dedicated to the women in my life. My three daughters Randi Storch Paul; Tracy Storch Schafer; Alysia Storch Carver; and my wife of 36 years Jeanne Klier Storch.

PROLOGUE, LEADING FROM BEHIND

The title of this book describes how a leaderless and rudderless nation is floundering.

One could call the messaging by the main character, or characters as the cover portrays, duplicitous -- that's because it is. You see if you are a passive progressive and lead from behind you are delivering mixed messages that are in conflict with one another and confusing at best to the people you serve.

That's what this book is all about, reflecting upon a period of six years that this nation has endured under President Barrack Hussein Obama, delivering a plethora of double oxymoron rhetoric.

"You can keep your doctor," only to find out you can't; "You can keep your insurance carrier," only to find out it's not possible.

"And the demonstration in Benghazi was over a film, according to Obama," when in fact it was a terrorist attack by al Qaida.

These are the classics of Obama's legacy that went beyond his promises of 'Hope and Change,' with his duplicitous political Teleprompter – perhaps that's why there were two – with Hollywood-like rhetoric and a signature legislative and foreign policy of mendacity.

The columns that follow record this period of time in satire. It is the only palatable form of delivery; because of its seriousness it needs to be reflected in some form of humor or one might break down in tears over the damage it has done to a nation.

But it's for real. It could even be a "paraprosdokian."

Paraprosdokian is Greek and means "beyond" and "expectation," the definition being for those, like me, who didn't know.

It is a figure of speech in which the latter part of a sentence requires the reader or listener to reinterpret the first part. It is not an oxymoron, but is frequently used by comedians and satirists.

Perhaps Obama should try using paraprosdokian for the delivery of his messages more often, for it could even be more confusing than an oxymoron and it would be an appropriate conclusion to his two remaining years of executing the late Saul Alinsky's playbook, based upon his book, "Rules for Radicals."

It should come as no surprise that polls report that President Obama has been deemed by the people to be the worst president of the United States since WW II.

This must make former President Jimmy Carter feel good to be displaced in this category, for Obama worked harder to earn this achievement than he did winning the Nobel Peace Prize.

And, it must make Mitt Romney feel bad because the same Gallop Poll found that people now believe he would have made a better president.

This poll, unlike others, is not based upon a day to day whim of opinion, but based upon the 6 year performance of O, now in his second term as president.

George W. has been bashed more than a Bush deserves to be, but his classy silence must have worn the O down, because there's less of it today than yesterday.

It is unlikely Obama will be able to turn around his negative legacy in the next two years and furthermore it doesn't appear that he wants to, or even cares.

He appears to be disengaged, more interested in golf then beheadings by ISIS or their threats against the United States or other nations building up military might, while we pull back on ours, and he seems to be non-pulsed by the cooling of relations with Russia.

On the domestic side of the pond, he arrogantly told House Speaker John Boehner, who is suing him over his misuse of executive privilege, violating the Constitution on Obamacare some 50 times, "So sue me."

The phone, the pen and executive order is the Alinsky, Marxist influence of the Obama unconstitutional game plan that fulfills his campaign promise of "Change," casting away the "Hope" only he has now in his own future delivering half-million-dollar speeches to those who may still want to hear his socialistic rhetoric.

A metaphorical poster of former President George W. Bush asks, "Miss me yet?'

You bet we do!

I have interspersed these readings with offbeat columns of the times so you wouldn't be beltway fatigued, including an epilogue and a tribute to my mentor.

Enjoy the read . . .

O DID HAVE AN ISIS STRATEGY ITS CODE NAME WAS "PIN THE NOTE"

Washington DC (Storch Report) September 16, 2014 — Obama did have a strategy for ISIS after all.

He revealed it at a private off the record meeting at the White House and the New York Times reported on it, but even though they had three representatives present, they claim they obtained the information from other unnamed sources that were present.

I guess there must have been multiple discussions going on at the same time at which the Times' reporters were not present.

So according to the anonymous sources the conversation went something like this:

J (Journalist): "Mr. President you must have had a strategy for ISIS even though you said you didn't?

O (Obama): "I did but unfortunately I couldn't reveal it because our lines of communications weren't open to ISIS."

J: "What was the strategy?"

O: "Well, the code name was, 'Pin the Note.' You see, ISIS made a major strategic error by beheading those two American journalists and the anger it generated resulted in the American public forcing me into taking military action."

J: "And what is it that you would have advised?"

O: "If I had been an adviser to ISIS I would not have killed the hostages but released them and pinned notes on their chests saying, 'Stay out of here; this is none of your business.' Such a move might have undercut support for military intervention and that would have pleased me. After all, I'm better at fund raising, than theater."

J: "Is it true that you are seeing Charles Krauthammer?"

O "I deny that I'm under therapy. Who does that Karut think he is calling me a narcissist . . . a psychiatrist? I don't, "talk like the emperor, Napoleon. I never put my hand inside my coat as Napoleon did. I don't think I'll invite him to the White House again."

J: "Napoleon or Krauthammer?"

O: "You know who I'm talking about, I talk to Napoleon all the time. In fact I had his fiddler here for a concert a few weeks ago."

J: Krauthammer said you used 'I' 29 times when you announced the killing of Osama bin Laden, is that true?

O:" I think it was 30, but I didn't pull the trigger."

I WOULD RATHER HAVE A SLOPPY JOE, THE NEW JERSEY SANDWICH

Newark NJ (Storch Report) September 4, 2014 — Yes, I'm going to declare that the Sloppy Joe sandwich originated in New Jersey and I'm not talking about that place named Sloppy Joe's in Cuba in the 30's, nor the one named after it in Key West frequented by Ernest Hemingway.

A Sloppy Joe is a cold delicatessen sandwich, not to be confused with that more common sandwich made from loose ground beef.

And if you grew up in New Jersey, as I did, in Irvington on the border of Newark in an area called Weequahic, where Phillip Roth the author grew up and had a lot of complaints according to his books, you can almost still smell Seymour Tabatchnick flavors wafting from his Deli, if only from your memory and senses, of fresh meat, bagels, lox and the smell of brine coming from the pickle barrel.

Tabatchnick said he invented the Sloppy Joe. I think he did, after all he invented a lot of tasty things that were of Jewish origin and everybody's likings, even frozen New York Style Chicken Broth that makes the common cold feel better, according to Jewish mothers.

I like to think I was the only gentile on the block in a Jewish neighborhood at the time where Jewish delis flourished. But I

wasn't, I had a family and they too were gentiles, and then there was the Polish lady that owned the apartment we lived in, but all of my friends were Jewish and we loved Tabatchnick's.

A Sloppy Joe is made up of meats of your choice and is always on a triple decker of rye bread with one or more types of sliced deli meat, such as ham, turkey, roast beef, corned beef, pastrami with Swiss cheese, coleslaw and Russian dressing.

You can't find a good Sloppy Joe outside of New Jersey.

Everybody likes to take credit for something good especially if it falls into the public domain and is a gastronomic delight. Take the cheese burger, which seems to belong to Jimmy Buffett because he sang a song about it and you can't believe the number of joints around the world that claim he coined it at their place, one is on Cabbage Key, a barrier reef not far from me.

I can't think of one sandwich that belongs to anyone else as the Sloppy Joe belongs to New Jersey.

There are many that want to take claim for it as they do salt water taffy from the Jersey Shore – no one goes to the beach in New Jersey they go to the 'Shore' – or the hot dog from Rut's Hut or Taylor Ham. Who eats Taylor Ham outside of New Jersey?

But even in New Jersey there are those who want to take claim to inventing the Sloppy Joe. The Town Hall Deli in South Orange claims to have invented the New Jersey Sloppy Joe in the 1930's. They say a Maplewood politician, Thomas Sweeney went on vacation to Cuba and frequented a bar named Sloppy Joe's from which the Key West bar got its name.

It seems the bar's owner laid out a variety of food fixings for patrons, who put sandwiches together. So when Sweeney came back he asked Town Hall to cater his poker games with the same sort of sandwiches and they caught on.

In the '50s, there were several Jewish delis in Newark and surroundings who were also selling the sandwich. Places like Tabatchnicks, Kartzman's, Union Pantry in Union; but today, the Millburn Deli in Millburn is one of the most famous and successful

of the Sloppy Joe providers and there is Mr. J's Deli in Cranford, who has labeled the ham version as a "Regular Joe."

The last Sloppy Joe I had was from the Towne Deli in Summit, and I can't find one here in Florida the way they make them in Jersey.

I still think the late Tabatchnick invented the Sloppy Joe. Seymour died in 2012 at the age of 91 and left quite a legacy. He opened 12 delicatessens, three deli restaurants, a manufacturing plant for meat provisions and a frozen soup factory, with some 24 varieties of soup. The deli's and restaurants are all gone.

But his frozen soups live on and you can still get his New York Style Chicken Broth, even here in Florida.

I would rather have a Sloppy Joe!

NOW IT'S SOCIAL MEDIA'S FAULT

Washington DC (Storch Report) September 2, 2014 — President Obama never seems to run out of people to blame for his failures.

I don't think he was ever very fond of Harry Truman, who once sat in the same oval office during World War II during the trials, tribulations and victories of the Greatest Generation of our time and said, the 'buck stopped' with him.

Over the weekend Obama, the silver slippery-tongued orator said while preaching to the Democratic choir, "the world has always been messy" and he thought Americans were unduly worried now because of Twitter, You Tube and the nightly news.

Did the leader of the free world with the most powerful military under his command really say that?

Somehow I think he actually forgot that President George W. Bush was still around.

Now what is it that he thinks America is unduly worried about?

Could it be that he admitted last Thursday that "we don't have a strategy" to combat ISIS in Iraq nor are we willing to take the fight to their headquarters in Syria?

Could it be that ISIS beheaded an American journalist a week ago upon which he commented while on vacation and then dashed off to play golf on Martha's Vineyard?

Could it be that today another American journalist was beheaded by ISIS, with the announcement coming at 1:05 PM and Obama vanished without comment at 3:40 PM?

Once again, I guess it's the social media and the news media's fault for logging in these facts.

Today it was revealed that Obama knew of ISIS rise as a terrorist threat in Iraq from daily briefings a year-ago while conveying to the public, he was caught off guard by a lack of Intel.

"In part, we're just noticing now because of social media and our capacity to see in intimate detail the hardships that people are going through," he said.

While preaching to the choir he said, "It feels like the world is falling apart . . . we've seen the barbarity of an organization like ISIL . . . We've seen divisions within the Muslim community between the Shia and Sunni.

"All of that makes things pretty frightening. And then, you turn your eyes to Europe and you see the President of Russia making a decision to look backwards instead of forward."

Then he rhetorically delivers a series of mixed metaphors to his congregation about American military superiority, how well the economy is doing and compares the current global situation favorably to the deprivations of the Great Depression.

Perhaps President Obama is paying too much attention to the social media on his iPhone, and not enough attention to his daily intelligence briefings on ISIS in Iraq and Syria

WHITE HOUSE MINOR LEAGUE TEAM ON THE ROAD DOING WHAT IT DOES BEST, FUNDRAISING

New York (Storch Report) August 4, 2014 — President Obama told the enemy this week that he doesn't have a strategy for ISIS or Syria for the grisly murders and atrocities they are carrying out in the Middle East and threatening to bring to the US and he was absolutely pellucid about it as he promised he would be six years ago.

ISIS knows full well he has a strategy for golf for shortly after he condemned ISIL for beheading a 40-year-old journalist, he had a 1 PM tee time at a Vineyard Golf Club. They also know that he has a penchant for fundraising and that he's pretty good at it.

So today while White House Press Secretary Josh Earnest was fielding the media flack at a press briefing answering questions from the previous day of Obama's strategic blundering disclosure and the Pentagon was scrambling to come up with a strategy that O said he didn't have, POTUS bordered Air Force One for fund raisers in New York and Rhode Island.

It's no secret that this is the Labor Day weekend. And, for the 250 persons and up in each venue who planned to pony up some $32,000 each to rub elbows with Obama in New York and Rhode Island it won't spoil their last fling of summer.

But for the other swells, perhaps of some other political persuasion, it throws a monkey wrench into their travel plans.

You see the FAA has issued a no-fly warning that extends for Friday and all day Saturday through Sunday grounding seaplanes to East Hampton, Montauk, Martha's Vineyard and Nantucket.

Well, I guess that's alright, the president had his vacation and he did so through multiple crises which didn't interrupt his plans.

After all $32,000 a pop is no small change, for the Dems coffers.

The thousands of dollars the small charters will loose on the busiest weekend of the year, well that's another story.

THE STRATEGY IS AT THE BOTTOM OF CUP WITH A FIST BUMP FOR A BIRD OR A PAR

Washington DC (Storch Report) August 28, 2014 – President Obama came up short of saying macabre terrorist acts in the Middle East, Russia aggressively invading Ukraine and threats from China were acts of 'workplace violence' and just admitted he didn't know what they were or have a 'strategy' for anything but picking up a golf ball from a plastic cup, and fist bumping his buddy Alonzo Mourning after a bird or a par.

It was refreshing, after all he has been promising transparency for six years and he finally delivered it admitting that he didn't know what he was doing 'yet.'

He of course didn't tell us what we didn't know, after all he just came off of a golfing vacation and things happened rather rapidly while he was gone: an American journalist was beheaded, a black was killed by a white police officer in Ferguson Mo. with six bullets, Russia invaded Ukraine, a Chinese jet did a Top Gun maneuver over international waters on top of a US surveillance plane and he barely had time to get out of his golfing attire into a beige tropical summer suit before the Labor Day weekend, after which he could no longer wear it and be fashionable, before addressing the nation on the terrorism threats of ISIS to the US.

As a matter of fact he didn't even have time to think of labeling all of this as nothing but 'workplace violence' as he did in the Ft. Hood terrorist massacre some years ago and capture all the villains we can collect and try them as ordinary criminals in the US.

He quickly told us he was not engaging in anything but golf and fund raising which will allow him to wear that summer suit two more times before the Labor Day weekend is over and then according to protocol it will be put away until next summer.

While golfing with Mourning, as in Alonzo, you know he's a part-owner of the Boston Celtics, Obama was overheard saying he does his best,' to stay away from red lines' as he did in Syria.

Alonzo said that he noticed, as Obama's golf ball trickled near an out of bounds 'red line' at the Vineyard Golf Club.

Obama, appearing more tanned and rested than usually, told us that Russia was being 'weakened' by its actions not strengthened, adding that the US will not take any military action to resolve the Ukraine situation.

There have been six rounds of Obama sanctions against Russia and somehow do not seem to be weakening the aggressor, while Obama, doesn't seem to have his strategy worked out, 'yet.'

As for Iraq, he claims the air strikes are working, but there is little evidence behind the declaration and there is no strategy for Syria.

Once again Obama assured us that on foreign and domestic policy, or for that matter on any other policy, he is swinging his Big Bertha from behind looking for support, for what, and no one knows not even him, while the varmints are scurrying off the sinking ship.

WE GOT THEM ONCE, WE CAN GET THEM AGAIN . . .

Washington DC (Storch Report) June 11, 2014— We now know that releasing five terrorists for a deserter in the army was a good thing and according to the Obama administration, "We have nothing to apologize for."

And, to think these five terrorists could possibly be a threat once again to Americans is "baloney," according to Secretary of State John Kerry.

And, if the terrorists prove to be a threat we can catch them again, or just Drone them dead.

Somehow no one is talking about what the toll might have been to our US military to capture them in the first place.

Obama thinks releasing coal in the atmosphere is more dangerous than releasing terrorists to kill again.

And Kerry believes climate change is America's most dangerous threat.

So, don't worry about those high value terrorists that were released from Gitmo that the Taliban is touting as a victory for the bad guys, Qatar is watching them. And if they somehow miss them, even though no one seems to know where they are now, we will get them once again.

I wouldn't suggest Americans be in the wrong place at the wrong time these days, nor take this trust to the bank.

Yesterday Josh Earnest, Obama's new press secretary designee, was asked what Hillary Clinton, former Secretary of State and wanabee candidate for president, and Obama's foreign policy achievements were, and he earnestly cited the withdrawal of troops from Iraq and ending the war there and shutting down the war in Afghanistan.

But he failed to mention that Iraq is on the verge of a civil war and the Taliban is poised to take over Afghanistan once we withdraw from there.

If these are achievements, the White House doesn't have very lofty goals.

BALONEY GETS A BAD RAP

Paris, France (Storch Report) June 9, 2014— I think Baloney gets a bad rap.

The slang word Baloney comes from the Bologna sausage which is traditionally made from the "odds and ends" of chicken, turkey, beef, or pork. It is an inexpensive deli meat and is often pronounced and spelled "baloney."

When John Kerry our esteemed Secretary of State was asked, "What do you say to the families of American soldiers that perhaps these guys (The five terrorists released from Gitmo in exchange for Sgt. Bergdahl) could go back and kill Americans again?' he said, "I just think that's a lot of Baloney, to be truthful with you. . ."

Apparently the slang word took off in the 1930's thanks to Alfred E. Smith, who served as the governor of New York four times and was the first Roman Catholic major party nominee to run for president. The word took on the connotation of foolish talk or nonsense. He often used the term "Baloney" in reference to Washington bureaucracy.

Kerry reached deep into his vocabulary bag of words for this one to put down the thought that once a terrorist always a terrorist who might just by chance kill again.

There's a lot of Baloney in DC and Smith apparently knew what he was talking about.

If Baloney is made up of "odds and ends" couldn't President Obama be Baloney, his mother was white and his father was black? Oh don't tell me that's racist, it's a fact . . . although a double entendre.

And, we certainly have seen a lot of nonsense and heard a lot of baloney since Barack Hussein Obama has been President for six years.

What appears to be nonsense is Kerry's inappropriate use of the word, for it is more likely that the terrorists will kill again than not, even though he used the word in France rather than Washington.

"I'm telling you they (the Qatar's) aren't the only ones keeping an eye on them," Kerry told CNN. "And we have confidence in those requirements. And if they're violated, then we have the ability to be able to do things."

That sounds like a bunch of "Baloney" to me.

HOCKEY, A GAME ABOUT A PUCK YOU CAN'T SEE

Los Angeles (Storch Report) June 8, 2014 — I watched the Stanley Cup last night as a non-hockey fan and I was rooting for New York against Los Angeles. I root for all NY sports teams, especially when they are playing LA.

I don't care for Hockey primarily because it's about a puck that burly guys with beards, that look like terrorists and sometimes behave like them, flick a one inch thick 3 inch in diameter disk made of vulcanized rubber with a stick at speeds up to 100 mph that I can't see. In fact the announcers of the game often report that the players can't see the puck either and I am sure the goalies will vouch for that too.

Now to make it perfectly clear as politicians might say, I'm watching the game on an 80 inch flat TV screen and I can see the puck when it's on the ice better than on a TV half the size. But when it goes airborne at 100 mph forget about it. I need to trust the replay and a freeze frame to believe what happened.

Now I must admit that I am in awe of the player's ability to skate backwards, I say this only because even I can skate forward. I'm also impressed with the player's speed on ice, they move like lacrosse players on grass handling the hockey stick and puck like a lacrosse player handles a stick and ball in a loose mesh pouch on the end of a stick.

I have never been a cold weather athlete, least of all someone that wanted to hit a doughnut with an L shaped stick on ice in below freezing temperatures.

I was once given a hockey stick signed by Wayne Gretzky, I was so impressed with it I gave it to a member of my family and warned them that I had good reason to believe the signature was forged. Otherwise, I would have donated it to be auctioned-off for charity.

The score in the third period was tied at 4-4, even though NY got off to a 2-0 lead as they did in the first game and lost, but I was still bored even though the announcers tried to make what was happening on ice more interesting than what I was seeing.

The game went into OT and LA scored to win once again 5-4.

Don't send me a ticket to watch a hockey game, I don't want to get hit in the head by something I can't see; I'd rather get excited watching curling.

DO WE HAVE A COMMANDER IN CHIEF IN THE UNITED STATES ANYMORE?

Washington DC (Storch Report) May 29, 2014 — Is the Commander in Chief still the President of The United States?

And, are they one and the same?

I get confused on the basis of what's being reported in the news today.

If the Commander in Chief is still the one that professes to have the backs of those serving in the military and those that have served, why are veterans dying because they have to wait 117 days to get a medical appointment in VA hospitals and why is a US Marine serving in a Mexican jail for two months because he made a wrong turn at the border with nary a word or aid from the Commander in Chief, President Barack Hussein Obama, or Vice President Joe Biden who was on a diplomatic mission in Mexico while the latter incident was unfolding?

I suppose this shouldn't come as any surprise when we have witnessed the Ambassador to Libya, Chris Stevens be slain along with three other diplomats by al Qaeda terrorists at a diplomatic outpost in Benghazi while the Commander in Chief didn't have their backs either.

In fact we didn't even know where the Commander in Chief was that night other than he was not in the White House Situation

Room where he should have been during an ongoing attack lasting seven hours. In contrast Obama was in that room for a photo op when the Navy Seals killed Osama bin Laden. Memos revealed as a result of the Benghazi investigation suggest Obama was most likely orchestrating cover-up talking points about a demonstration over a negative Islamic film to protect his reelection campaign at the time while he was falsely claiming al Qaeda was decimated.

Over the weekend the Commander in Chief made a surprise visit to Afghanistan for a PR staged tribute to our troops and while doing so his administrative staff outed the CIA Station Chief in Afghanistan; he can't even protect the back of our Intel officers in harm's way, least of all our military or diplomats. He is in charge of an administrative staff that can't shoot straight domestically or abroad.

Then he manages to get home in time to address warriors graduating from West Point to deliver a disjointed sophomoric speech that informs graduates that US foreign policy in the future will rely on the cooperation of NATO and direction from the UN, the most impotent organization ever created.

The graduating warriors were also told they would more likely be fighting climate warming than conflicts on foreign soil.

But he assured them, he was not a weak president, contrary to public opinion.

I wouldn't want to be in a fox hole with this Commander in Chief, least of all meeting him on the beaches of Normandy.

Semper fi!

O: 'I DON'T KNOW'

Washington DC (Storch Report) May 21, 2014 – The response to every scandal that now sits before President Obama in the Oval Office is, "I don't know."

It reminds me of Bill Cosby's classic skit about his children and the lead line that, "All children have brain damage."

Cosby comes into the room with a Coke. He sets it down and reaches for his newspaper. His child comes in and grabs the drink.

Cosby says gimme that! Didn't I tell you not to drink it? The child says "Uhh Huh." He says, what did I just say? "You said but for not to not you drink."

The skit goes on in this vain and the kid continues to reach for the drink. Finally Cosby says, after the kid picks it up again and starts to drink the Coke and he says gimme that! Didn't I just tell you to . . . ahhhh . . . Well why did you do it?

"I don't know."

Every scandal sitting on the desk of President Obama that now consists of Benghazi, Fast & Furious, IRS, NSA spying on the world, the FBI spying on reporters and now the VA scandal of killing veterans by delaying medical appointments results in Obama and his spokespersons saying, "I don't know," much like the Cosby skit of brain damaged children.

Obama knows nothing, when we know he knows everything.

He is not brain damaged, his policies are brain deranged and he is a master of deception, despite the fact the nation knows he spoke out on the VA issue in 2008, but claims he only heard of the issue in recent weeks from news reports. And, has yet to speak out on the scandal.

He has the experience of a child, and often delivers a spin of one with the defense of he didn't know.

But now we hear from his Chief of Staff that Obama is madder than just being mad, as his Secretary of the Veterans Administration, Erick Shinseki said.

Both should be accountable for this latest of scandals in O's administration, but once again stonewalling seems to be the strategy for handling scandals. But I know, why he says, "I don't know," Bill Cosby told me.

DID CHELSEA GET PREGNANT FOR HILLARY?

New York (Storch Report) April 27, 2014 — There's been a lot of speculation over Chelsea Mezvinsky's pregnancy and whether she did it for Mom, Hillary, as in Clinton?

I think all of this speculation is absolutely absurd. Imagine timing your sex and birth of a baby to advance your mother's political career? I mean after all what advantage would it give to someone running for president to be called 'granny,' after all isn't Hillary old enough already?

It's not like sex was something that Bill and Hillary thought a lot about together; now Bill . . . well, that's another story.

But to think, as some are suggesting, that they would plot such a union for political purposes and have the birth come in the midst of a presidential campaign to benefit Mom and distract from Hillary's negatives, is just not the type of Clinton family that we have witnessed during their years in the White House, or public service to our nation.

Nevertheless the mouthpiece of liberals, the New York Times asks, "Does the word 'grandmother' connote authority, durability and wisdom, or a less-flattering set of associations?"

And, Politico another liberal leaning voice declares, "the baby announcement 'a politico-obstetric earthquake,' high on the

Richter scale . . . and fraught with meaning for Hillary: "Clinton will be something else entirely: the most prominent American politician ever to become a grandmother. As far as sympathetic roles go, it doesn't get much better than that."

And the announcement has already caused an ideological royal cultural fervor when Ted Cruz aide Amanda Carpenter tweeted: "I love days like this when everyone recognizes a baby is a baby and not a fetus."

They are already speculating that the new baby will be on the campaign bus and Hillary won't have to be hugging and kissing strangers' babies, she will have one of her own to cuddle and kiss.

And let's be realistic, Hillary as the globetrotting Secretary of State with little accomplishments, doesn't need her grandchild to cover-up Benghazi, she has already got that issue out of the way by calling that terror attack the "biggest regret" on her watch.

And those facetious, cynical, sarcastic Tea Party righteous conservatives should not be calling for Monica Lewinsky to be the Godmother.

IF I WERE PRESIDENT AND GOING ON TRIP TO ASIA . . .

JAPAN (Storch Report) April 25, 2014 – If I were president, you know like Barack Hussein Obama, and I were going on a trip to Asia to buttress my foreign relations in this region, I would pray to God Almighty for the following stories and headlines:

- **Obama's trip to Asia on Earth Day takes him to the West Coast and will generate 568,032 pounds of carbon emissions, then he will travel to Asia generating another 1,169,248 pounds of carbon emission — and unfortunately for earth, he will have to come back.**
- **When he arrives in Japan he has a $300 a plate Sushi dinner in one of the most expensive restaurants in Japan.**
- **Then he bows to a robot in Japan and says it was scary.**
- **Then the mouth piece of the Obama administration, the New York Times headlines on page one, "Obama Suffers setbacks in Japan and the Mideast."**
- **He then goes on to South Korea for a week and North Korea threatens to conduct its fourth nuclear test**
- **Meanwhile President Vladimir Putin of Russia increases tensions in the Ukraine, sending Russian jets into the region**

> **and Obama throws out another 'manhood threat' that further sanctions are 'teed up.'**

This is but the beginning of his Asian trip without a stop in China, more to come.

WHAT IS MANHOOD . . . IS THAT LIKE A MACHO THING?

Washington DC (Storch Report) April 24, 2014 – The word Manhood came into play this week on a Sunday talk show when David Brooks a columnist for the New York Times brought it up in reference to President Obama and his stand in the Middle East and the Ukraine on NBC's Meet the Press and apparently he thinks the president is getting a bad rap.

Nevertheless that's Obama's perception in the Middle East according to Brooks . . . "And let's face it, Obama, whether deservedly or not, does have a — I'll say it crudely — but a manhood problem in the Middle East. Is he tough enough to stand up to somebody like Assad or somebody like Putin? I think a lot of the rap is unfair, but certainly in the Middle East there is an assumption that he's not tough enough."

I guess it's a Macho thing, big men that ride horses don't eat $300-dollar-a-plate Sushi in Japan with little people.

Obama is more of a dove than a hawk, since he has been president he has pulled out of one war, is withdrawing from another and refuses to engage in a new one but is quick to 'draw the line in the sand' which quickly fades with time in the winds of Middle East conflict.

Aside from it being a perception thing it also appears to be a global cultural thing. Since Obama has been in office his policies

seem to be bent on leveling the playing field. Domestically he wants nationalism to replace capitalism, he wants socialism to replace democracy, a president to be anointed King and the constitution to be replaced with orders from a monarchy.

Equal pay for equal work, redistribution of wealth, a society where everyone is a winner and no one is a looser. Or, another way of looking at it there are no winners, everyone is a looser.

When there are global conflicts such as those that are taking place in the Ukraine, where one country Russia under President Vladimir Putin is taking over another, or Syria where President Bashar Assad is committing human atrocities in the hundreds of thousands, Obama believes these issues should be resolved with diplomacy. He has earned the perception well.

Further steps, Obama believes, would be leveling the playing field by marginalizing the most powerful military in the world, the United States Military. And he has already taken steps in this direction. He wants to remove the peace a powerful military represents and the word exceptionalism from America's vocabulary.

Capitalism breeds competition, nationalism, or big government, feeds dependency. We need not look too far to see the seeds of discontent, disruption, discord, dishonesty and failure in the socialism behind Obamacare.

The will to win has been taken out of the youth of America. To play T Ball with no winners or losers is not worth the parent's time to watch. To hide with no one to seek is not a game. Sport with no winners, no losers = no fun. To learn to win is as important as to learn to lose.

Competition is an important ingredient in life whether it be academics, business, technology, politics, diplomacy, wars, or the prevention thereof.

According a recent study in Britain a generation of children is no longer interested in winning on the sporting field.

Research showed that the majority of children are not bothered if the competitive element is removed from football, cricket,

rugby and hockey, saying playing for fun or being with friends is more important.

The same culture is taking over the youth of America and perhaps it is being learned because we no longer have Macho leaders in the United States or those that display manhood to nations that respect what a threat means and fear the result that it could bring under a forceful leader and powerful military.

Perhaps Macho Men don't eat Sushi because many died of Minamoto disease years ago from eating raw fish from polluted waters in Japan. But then again, I don't believe it was gourmet blue-Fin Tuna at $300-a-plate.

A GIFT OF SEEDS OF HYPER-LIBERALISM TO THE POPE?

Rome It (Storch Report) March 27, 2014 -- President Obama in his audience today with Pope Francis gave the Pontiff a chest of seeds, both fruit and vegetables, from the White House 'Defeat Garden' as opposed to the once known 'Victory Gardens' we had during World War II.

The chest was custom-made of leather and reclaimed wood from Baltimore's Basilica of the National Shrine of the Assumption of the Blessed Virgin Mary, one of the oldest Catholic cathedrals in the US, and inscribed with the date of their meeting.

I wonder if the seeds were blessed with slimness or hyper-liberalism, or a smattering of both?

If I were the Pope I would be careful of their use and to whom he feeds the bounty.

FROZEN LLADRO'S IN THE AISLES OF PUBLIX

Englewood Fl (Storch Report) March 25, 2014 -- I went to Publix to pick up some Kobe burgers they were holding for me today and I never saw so many old people frozen in place.

It was about 10:30 AM and I thought they were taking their afternoon nap in mid-morning.

I wanted to run into them with my shopping cart, but I was afraid there would be broken pieces of Lladro' figurines all over the floor.

Perhaps they got AM confused with PM that happens a lot down here in Florida.

Sometimes I think the crop of old snowbirds we got this winter are still frozen from the cold winter they had up North. Perhaps they should make a gradual descent South so they at least thaw-out before they arrive.

The people that check you out are as old as those that get frozen in place in the aisles.

And when the baggage guy winds up with faulty plastic bags it's a real problem that takes some time to resolve.

Because it now seems they are awake and preparing for the early bird special.

I like old people, after all I'm one of them; I just wish they would get their brake lights fixed, especially when they decide to stop pushing their shopping carts to take a nap.

Oh, my choice of the Lladro on the top of this column? I thought it would draw some attention, I didn't see anything like it while shopping for my Kobe burgers.

WHITE MEN CAN'T PLAY BASKETBALL

Manasota Key FL (Storch Report) March 25, 2014 -- I know white men can't jump, a movie told me that.

While watching March Madness — that's the college basketball tournament that is dominating your TV set today — I can't find any white men on the court.

I think this wealth redistribution has gone too far.

Is it really Obama again?

I'm really getting tired of those that don't let him win?

His basketball career is much like his political career, no experience, few swishes and too many misses.

I would like to see equal opportunity in basketball, much like the blacks wanted to see it in baseball yesterday.

It is one thing not being able to jump, but not being able to play is another. I thought in this socially correct society everyone makes the team, everyone is a winner and everyone goes home with a trophy.

There is something wrong. Today there is nothing but black on black, what happened to skins v shirts? Or, white on white?

Does anyone know where I can watch a curling match?

DOES THE DIN OF THE SOCIAL NETWORK JIBBERJABBER IMPACT AMERICA'S PRODUCTIVITY?

Manasota Key Fl (Storch Report) March 17, 2014 -- We like to believe that Twitter and Facebook and other social networks improve communications among us, but when carefully examining the content of the messages transmitted, for the most part, it's hardly informative or productive.

But it does provide us with the 'choices' President Obama's liberal policies have given us through entitlements while 10.5 million Americans are unemployed and now have the 'choice' to communicate the mundane to others in the same state of mind with nothing to do.

Social networks are filled with pictures of kids, families, and dog's events, comments about politics, TV shows, likes, dislikes, places, food, desserts, frustrations and whereabouts. Some comments are ugly as are some dogs, especially those frothing from the mouth. Then there are the dogs and kids that do tricks or performances set up by their producer-parents and post them on YouTube.

Do we really care?

I don't, but I guess some do enjoy the non-productive, non-informative trivia, for I guess it passes the time when you're unemployed.

Then there are those that post where they are like sunning in St. Tropez, dinning and sightseeing in Paris or skiing in the Alps while drawing envy from 'friends.' They write much the way they do when delivering their annual year-end missiles of achievements, goodness and places visited, but fail to deliver the bad or the ugly.

I post headlines of news stories and columns to promote my website and I offer birthday wishes to family and friends on Twitter which is picked up on Facebook – but nothing personal. That doesn't make me better than anyone else that tells more, I just don't find trivia to be relevant to anything as I don't find President Obama relevant to much nor as transparent as some of my friends. But this subject did give me an opportunity to trash him once again.

GRUMPY OLD MANASOTA KEY MAN WANTS SNOWBIRDS TO GO HOME

Manasota Key Fl (Storch Report) March 11,2014 --While the Snowbirds that invaded this tiny island on the west coast of Florida this year were tired of the snow where they selected to live, I'm tired of them encroaching upon my piece of paradise where I selected to live.

The traffic is bumper to bumper coming onto the island and going off. A two mile trip off and back on the island could be a two our adventure dodging the walkers, runners, bikers, the open draw bridge and the poor driving habits of the of old farts from the snow belt.

A trip to Publix, the local super market, is a dodge-em adventure in the parking lot.

A local can't get into the restaurants without reservations, where they take them, and the same places beg us for our business in the off season.

The prices go up in season and down in off season.

If I wanted to endure crowds I would have moved to Longboat Key or Siesta Key in Sarasota. But some 30 years ago I discovered Manasota Key and moved here.

You see according to the United States Census Bureau Manasota Key consists of 2.7 square miles of which, 1.1 square miles is land

and 1.7 square miles of it is water. I wish the snowbirds would spend more time in the water. Our population on the key is 1,345 with 769 households.

We have had notable residents on the island: Tim McGraw, country singer, Bobby Vinton, pop singer, are here and the late Donna Summer, singer/songwriter was here. The Vanderbilt's lived here when the island only had a dirt road and a portion at the north end still is only accessible by a dirt road. Dan Rowan of Rowan Martin fame lived and died here. And we once had two nudist camps here.

I am not going to give you the exact coordinates of where we are, but it doesn't matter – we've been found.

Next month the big boat races are coming to the island and will bring to us a parade, a bikini contest, off shore races and 25,000 people. The people will park on the mainland and be shuttled on and off in buses. I have press credentials and am looking forward to covering the events, but not the hordes of people.

If I am lucky the race course will take the boats by my house overlooking the Gulf of Mexico which will be viewable from my second floor deck.

We once, a decade or so ago, were invaded by Cubans trying to escape Dictator Castro, but they were rounded up by immigration authorities then; I don't know what they would do today. I do have some 200 palm trees that need trimming yearly.

This too will all pass in a few months or so and the island will be returned to its inhabitants. But you won't find this grumpy old man yelling from the rooftops, 'Com'on Down.'

THERE ARE JOBS FOR OBAMA & HIS ADMINISTRATION — THERE'S A SHORTAGE OF CLOWNS

Washington DC (Storch Report) February 18, 2014 -- The United States is running out of clowns – the real ones that make kids laugh. But there is an abundance of them in the Obama administration that the industry could tap into, but whether they could be funny is questionable, but they are child-like.

The clown trade organization could work their way down from President Obama and solve the Nation's multiple problems by giving him another job, but Vice President Joe, foot in mouth, Biden is probably much funnier, bumbling along as a distraction for Obama's failed policies.

There has been a 28% loss of clowns according to the World Clown Association.

I mean, where we are going to go when the call goes out to 'Send in the Clowns?'

To be a real clown is no longer cool, but it sure seems to be taking hold among our politicians.

Imagine, the industry could tap into the work force of the White House, move on to the Senate then to Congress and work their way through the Cabinet and the bungling Secretary of

States' and Health and Human Resources and wrap up with the attorney general, the IRS and the head of NSA.

All have achieved the Peter Principal by being promoted to a position beyond their competence.

At least by demoting them to the level of clowns we could place them in a job in which perhaps they could achieve. At least they would be at a level of their competence and as a result resolve the problems of the clown trade and the nations' Juggernaut of a snail's pace of an economic recovery, Obamacare, and jobs.

With politicians as clowns perhaps then we could laugh-a-lot and not take any of them seriously, thus eliminating the impact they are taking on the lives of the people.

DOLLS ON ICE

Sochi Russia (Storch Report) February 9, 2014 -- I couldn't help but wonder while watching the female ice skating competitions tonight at the Sochi Olympics of where they find those diminutive, boob-less bodies, painted doll-like faces, glittering costumes, and attractive booties, to do impossible anatomical contortions on a slippery surface balancing on thin blades of steel to movements that capture the grace of the music they dance to.

While I'm in awe of the females that grace the ice with their talents, I am also amazed that I got through the maze of words I selected to put together for the lead to describe what I saw, even though I ended a sentence with a preposition.

My high school English teacher would have been proud of me despite the grammatical fopax.

But back to the dolls. Did you ever think how interesting skating could be if it focused on falls and recoveries following a failed double or triple axel?

It would be much the way the late Jim McKay use to report it when he used to say, "The thrill of victory and the agony of defeat." We could wrap up both by capturing victory from the jaws of defeat.

In this form of skating the focus would be on the failure of the jump, but the success of the recovery.

Perhaps we could even add some meat and boobs to the skater's figures, leaving the booties alone and giving them a wholesome look rather than Barbie faces.

And, we could carry the competition through the glossary of figure skating terms falling and recovering through the camel spin, the Choctaw turn, or candle stick spiral, Lutz or quadruple jump and twizzle.

After all, it might be more exciting than curling.

SMIDGEON

New York (Storch Report) February 8, 2014 -- I don't know about you but I can't think of when I last used the word 'smidgeon.' I think I knew what it meant when I was a tike. But I probably didn't know then what a tike meant.

It's not often that the word smidgeon comes into play in a sentence. Think about it, when was the last time you used the word? Perhaps, if you are a Chef using salt in a recipe you would use the word pinch of something to put in your creation, and smidgeon could be a substitute for pinch.

Well, since the Super Bowl was such a dud, President Obama put smidgeon back in play in a 10 minute pre-game interview with Bill O'Reilly of Fox News and I would suspect he is sorry he ever used the word.

And I'll bet the Scots are happy that O brought some notoriety back to the word, because most wordsmiths believe the Scots were the origin of the word.

O is a wordsmith, that's why he is where he is; it's certainly not because of experience or capability, which he has demonstrated the lack of in the past five years.

According to internet research, smidgeon is a diminutive and refers to a small amount of something. It's semantically cohesive with small. If it's not being used metaphorically to refer to something nonphysical, than it's either a small fragment of a solid or small amount of granular material.

During the O'Reilly interview O said that there was "not even a smidgeon of corruption" involved in the Internal Revenue Service's targeting of conservative groups.

When O heard of the IRS targeting conservatives he called it "outrageous" and said he would get to the bottom of this.

At a hearing in May Lois Lerner, who was in charge of the IRS's tax-exempt organization division, apologized for the agency's handling of conservative groups and later invoked the Fifth Amendment and resigned her post in September.

One doesn't invoke the Fifth without protecting themselves from potential culpability or corruption. Yet the O said there was not a smidgeon of corruption in the IRS scandal for which the Justice Department said to the Wall Street Journal that it was not pursuing any criminal charges, when the investigation of same is not complete.

Research on the word smidgeon indicated that there was also a relationship to the word "smudge" which comes from one or more of those diminutives.

I found the photo of O and Chris Matthews of NBC with a smidgeon of a smudge on his nose and thought it was symbolic.

SCIENTISTS SEARCHING FOR GLOBAL WARMING HUNG UP IN A PENGUIN ICE ESCAPADE

Antarctic (Storch Report) January 3, 2014 -- I got it from reliable sources in the Antarctic that a collation of penguins will be petitioning the UN to prevent any further research into the region by scientists trying to prove the premise of global warming.

After a Russian research ship, carrying climate warming scientists, became entrapped in ice; two ice breakers tried to save them, one failed, a helicopter was sent in to rescue the passengers and they were flown off a patch of ice onto another ice breaking ship, which is now also entrapped in ice, and the penguins are now concerned for the first time about global warming as a result of the carbon foot print left in the region as a result of the attempted rescue.

It was erroneously reported that Al Gore was on the ship, but he was on his jet heading for St Bart's.

Meanwhile in America a Nor'easter was moving up the east coast, collided with a cold front coming in from the west causing a massive winter storm dumping more than 22 inches of snow in New England and dropping temperatures into the minus column.

And following up this weather, all of which began with the research cutter becoming entrapped on Christmas Eve in Antarctic ice, another arctic blast is now coming in from the Midwest for the weekend and wind-chill temperatures in areas of North Dakota and Minnesota are predicted to be minus 50 degrees by the weekend.

While all of this was going on today, a study was published in the journal Nature by scientists that say the world's climate warming is faster than feared. Some even projected that eventually Miami would be under water and Key West would no longer exist. Globally, according to figures released in December by the United States National Climatic Data Center, 2013 was set to be the fourth hottest year in 134 years of records behind 2010, 2005 and 1998.

Fifty two of the passengers on board the Russian ship with alphabet letters on its bow for a name, are now on their second ship surrounded by ice, the crew of 22 on the first ship is looking for a thaw from those scientists predicting global warming before the ice crushes the ship's hull.

Try and sell global warming today to those in North Dakota, Minnesota, Chicago and areas of New England, but the penguins in Antarctic, I know, are concerned over that carbon footprint left in their land.

They plan to present their petition in formal attire to the UN in New York, sometime in August of this year.

Oh, I forgot to mention that some of the climate warming scientists suggested that their ship was entrapped by 'old ice' not new ice.

That's probably why the penguins are planning to come to New York in August rather than January.

BANANA REPUBLIC ARE US

Manasota Key Fl (Storch Report) December 23, 2013) -- When it sounds like someone honking to attract a duck, by someone looking like Jesus, lives in a swamp, drives a truck, talks like a born again redneck singing praises to God, is so attractive to our society's social network that it has legs among our media, it must be that we have found the Banana Republic that will rush to the internet to sign-up for Obamacare.

I guess I just don't get what attracts one to a man's fuzz on the face, least of all a beard that makes one look like they are playing for the House of David baseball team.

All of this, in my opinion, is taking a hair shirt beyond comprehension.

And, the media quacks and quacks about Duck Dynasty and its patriarch star Phil Robertson who delivered a slur denigrating gays allegedly based upon his religious beliefs, stands by it, and is challenging the A&E network that airs the show and suspended him for his redneck beliefs, like it was something new that they didn't know about when they signed him up for the reality show.

Now it appears to me that the media has been sucked in by a bunch of rednecks and a network taking advantage of a good publicity stunt. Millions have been made by this show, by both the rednecks and the network. Do you really think A&E network is going to walk away from all of this designed hype, perhaps created by a PR flack?

Welcome to the land of Herman Wouk's Kinja.

OBAMA HELD HIS YEAR-END PRESS CONFERENCE TODAY. A SUMMARY: BLAH, BLAH, BLAH

Washington DC (Storch Report) December 20, 2013 -- There was extra hot air coming out of the White House chimneys as President Obama bloviated to the media promising to be nicer to them in a New Year's resolution.

He was first asked if this was the worst year of his presidency.

He side-stepped the bluntness of the question by saying, "I don't think about it that way."

I'll bet he doesn't, or he wouldn't be sleeping at night, and there is no evidence he is.

He cast the question off to 'polls' saying "there will be ups and downs." Then he lectured the insular reporter that asked the question.

This accomplishes two objectives: it takes up time so there are fewer questions allowed, and it takes up time so there are fewer questions allowed.

The journalists he was to select to ask a question, he said, was based upon press secretary Jay Carney's judgment of who in the past year 'was naughty or nice.'

It was probably the most honest statement Obama made all year, you see he can do it despite what the naysayers say about his tendency to lie.

Then he shocked everyone by calling on Ed Henry of Fox News who took advantage of the opportunity with several follow-ups.

He said to Ed that his biggest mistake was the Obamacare roll-out admitting that there were not enough lines of authority, but then in defense he said, 'but we have more than 2 million sign ups,' much less than needed and much less than projected at this time.

When Henry got into NSA spying activities Obama seemed to rile when Ed compared him to Clapper who lied in his Congressional testimony on the subject. Obama responded, 'you're conflating me and Clapper.' I didn't quite understand this response, because both lied and Obama has more Pinocchio's.

Well, there wasn't much more worthy of talking about, it was more of the same issues with more of the same Blah answers.

Obama and his family then bordered a plane to Hawaii for his Christmas vacation.

He was bid Aloha by the Washington press corps.

TYING THE KNOT

ManasotaKeyFL(StorchReport)December13,2013--Therearemany interpretations of the phrase tying the knot, but the one that I am going to deliver a commentary on is a satirical one on the knot on a tie below a man's Adams' Apple perhaps a forerunner of another knot Eve encouraged to be tied.

I have been observing everyone from male President's, TV anchors and celebrities for longer than I would like to admit, about how they tie their ties and whether the dimple appears in the right place on the tie below the Adams Apple.

There have been dimples over the years that have appeared on men's and women's cheeks of both places and others of the anatomy that have been attractive to the opposite sex.

I really don't know if this applies to men's ties. But, I do know what looks spiffy in men's dress-wear and I don't know if the dimple in a tie attracts women, but it is sure noticed in Gentleman's Quarterly.

It is extraordinary that a high percentage of men do not know how to tie a knot in their tie. There are but a few that do.

I do not want to point out those that consistently do it correctly v those that don't. I want to be constructive to all my readers.

Therefore the knot that is most widely used is called the 'Four in Hand'; the only other knot that I know of is the Windsor, and I think that went out in style with the Duke and high buckled shoes.

And so let's begin with getting to the perfect knot in a tie with one dimple.

When I was the head of a major corporate PR department for some 20 years, a number of the top executives would walk into my office, close the door and ask two questions: where do I get my shirts cleaned and pressed like yours and how do I tie the knot in my tie the way you do?

It had nothing to do with the issues at hand or my job description. It had to do with the way I looked and they say that is one of the highest forms of flattery. But you see it didn't apply to what the ongoing image crises of the corporation or my responsibilities to contain them, were at the time, it had to do with the ego and appearance of those on a fast track to achieve their own goals.

It was then that I knew I had longevity, if I wanted it, over the egos of a knot, under the collar of CEO Wannabees.

Nevertheless, I still resigned from that corporation and moved on with them and other Fortune Five corporate entities in my own newly formed PR Consultancy, but the knot question continued to prevail, all among other management crises.

And, so now I want to pass along my secret to all from which to benefit about the knot in the tie with a singular dimple.

First of all do have a crisp clean shirt with a collar with no rumples or wrinkles — or fire your dry cleaner.

The tie must be a quality made tie, whether expensive or not, and that I assure you is possible.

There must be a degree of bulk to the tie in order to tie a good knot, but not too much because bulk in the wrong place can get in the way of a good knot. Before you buy the tie try tying it on and see if you can get a dimple in the knot and see how it lies on the chest. If you don't like what you see, put it back on the rack, if it's a quality tie it won't wrinkle.

Keep in mind that the $85 and up tie that you can buy in Manhattan can be gotten for much less elsewhere.

Now let's get to the bottom line of the knot in the tie with the dimple.

Put the tie underneath your crisp collar, make sure the right and left lengths are appropriately aligned, the left being shorter than the right if you are right handed, then do your four hand roll over slipping the fat part of the tie through the loop.

Now this is the important part . . . slowly slip through the loop then put your index finger in the middle of the tie to create one dimple only, and then gently and slowly slip the tie under your collar making sure it is centered and tight. You do not want two or three dimples in the knot, you want just one. No dimple is verboten.

And so, this is my bi-partisan knot tip for males to look cool for the New Year that is if you select to wear a tie!

NO SELFIE RESPECT

Africa (Storch Report) December 11, 2013 -- First came Obama's handshake with Castro then the assisted Selfie with Scandivian hottie Helle Thorning-Schmidt the Danish leader and Prime Minster David Cameron of the UK, at Nelson Mandel's Memorial Service while First Lady Michelle tried to ignore the photo op in which she was excluded with glum disdain.

It must have been a long trip home.

Facebook should declare Obama King of the Selfie generation. After all he earned this title more than the Nobel Peace Prize.

At the White House he does much of the same when he can get away with his own self staged Selfie's.

He tries to exclude photo journalists in nonpublic events, allowing only the official White House photographer to take pictures of him which are then fed, with prior approval, to the media as flack handouts.

Perhaps he will be taking his own Selfies now that he has experience.

All events during the Obama administration are staged, with a mixed racial civilian/military background choreographed to the theme of the subject and venues. Some of the props even faint.

The presidency today is made up of a series of Hollywood-like theatrics, rhetoric with little substance of policy or leadership.

This is evident by an ongoing campaign trail which he hasn't gotten off of since he was first elected president.

Three years after ObamCare became law he is still on the campaign trail to sell a failed program and policy. Now his 'Obama minions' are declaring Obamacare a racial slur created by wealthy whites.

Up until now we have seen a mixture of rhetoric, lies, golf and vacations interspersed with the underpinnings of an Alinsky ideology of wealth redistribution.

While the Selfie has now become part of the Obama administration and the solemn memorial service is not out of bounds for its use, the president has set a new standard of behavior that doesn't require dignity or respect.

THE WRONG TURKEY GOT PARDONED TODAY AT THE WHITE HOUSE

Washington DC (Storch Report) November 27, 2013 -- Popcorn the Turkey was pardoned today by President Obama at the White House . . . it should have been the other way around.

You got it, the wrong Turkey was pardoned.

While the Obamacare death panel spared the life of a Turkey today, don't expect the same for you under the Affordable Care Act. While a couple of Turkey's were spared today do you know how many were slaughtered that the nation will be feasting upon tomorrow? Just about as many Americans that have lost their health care insurance plans as a result of Obamacare, with about 80 million more to come.

President Obama came into office on a charismatic cloud filled with grandiose rhetoric and when the rhetoric didn't transcend into positive action, the people lost their trust in him.

Today 53 % of the nation do not believe he is honest.

There were early signs of his disingenuous, especially five years ago when he made his 09' world tour apologizing for US past actions and behavior. This apology tour reflects today upon his foreign policy with a single theme of dishonest rhetoric.

Obamacare is symbolic of a philosophical character of the president whose focus is on global wealth and power redistribution.

No single action of the president embodies this philosophy more that the ACA, the signature legislative accomplishment of Obama and it is imploding from within its own failed socialistic policies.

It is a plan for the greater good, but it is based upon a Ponzi scheme. In order for Obamacare to work the young must sign up to pay for the old, and the elderly must die before they necessarily should, in order for the system to pay for itself.

The failure of the Obamacare website is but a canard, a minor flaw of a failed concept that is proving that it can't work even if the website was functioning, but it in itself involves policies that were designed to self-destruct under the principles of capitalism.

The administration had three years to make ACA work. But you can't make something work that is flawed from the outset, and furthermore if you deliver multiple lies to make it work and are caught in those lies such as you, 'can keep your insurance plan, period' and you 'can keep your doctor, period' and you don't keep those promises you are not only Pinocchio, you are a Turkey.

Obama said the penalty involved in the ACA mandate if not followed by the taxpayer was not a tax, it was a fine, and the Supreme Court determined it was a tax. Another lie. Obama said Obamacare was not redistribution of wealth, the New York Times, the mouthpiece of the administration, recently said it was. Another lie.

And so if the Congress and the public knew of these lies, ACA would not have passed and if the electorate knew of these lies before the 2012 election Obama would not have been reelected to a second term.

Reflect upon the scandals that took place over the past five years: Fast and Furious, Benghazi, the FBI spying on journalists, and the IRS targeting conservative groups for political purposes, NSA spying on US citizens and the world, and the cover-ups within

each of these scandals and how many more lies were delivered by an administration that promised transparency, and you should be appalled.

This, to date, has been an administration of rhetoric and mendacity.

As I said, the wrong Turkey was pardoned today.

CARNEY SITCOM . . . NO, YOU CAN'T KEEP YOUR DOCTOR EITHER

Washington DC (Storch Report) November 19, 2013 -- President Obama promised Americans that they can keep their insurance, period. We found that statement wasn't true and the president apologized for misleading the people. Today Jay Carney, once again danced through his daily sitcom and in effect said you might not be able to keep your doctor either in response to a question.

But you see, it's not because the president misspoke, it's the way the insurance industry works. It 'churns,' that's a favorite word of cagey Carney, much like the process by which you make butter.

The insurance policies change from year to year, policies are canceled, and policies are modified. Some doctors are in others are out, it depends upon the policy you pick as to whether or not you can keep your doctor.

Does this mean the president is going to modify this lie? I wouldn't hold your breath, it's the insurance industry's fault.

Obama is taking so many steps backward he received a 55% failing grade on his job approval report card today, so much that he didn't have time to go to the ceremonies honoring the 150th anniversary of Lincoln's Gettysburg Address. The report from the

White House was that he was too busy dealing with the Obamacare website.

Obama purports to be a fan of Lincoln, he even said once that history will compare him to one of four presidents and Lincoln was one. He took the oath of office on a Lincoln bible during his inauguration, but failed to live up to the oath of the constitution on that bible.

He even once delivered the Gettysburg Address in Lincoln's words, but he left out God from his version of the speech.

Carney was an hour late for his press briefing – so what else is new – because he wanted to get the latest on the president's meeting with Senators on the Iran negotiations. There was nothing new, they broke down last week and they were beginning new negotiations tomorrow in Switzerland. The US position didn't change, Carney just reiterated them. When asked what Senators were present for the update, Carney wouldn't tell the press. So much for transparency.

Back to the website. Did you know they are working on it 24/7 except for spending time at hearings on Capitol Hill caused by the obstructionist GOP holding hearings on Obamacare and why it's not working?

Obama at another venue promoting Obamacare, revealed that it was a, "Difficult political environment," and that nobody is "doing very well according to the people."

I guess he was referring to his 55% disapproval rating.

Referring to the GOP Obama said that one side was investing in failure. I don't know if this is true or not, but I do know the other side is achieving failure.

On another subject it was revealed today by the New York Post that the Department of Labor was cooking the books a month prior to Obama's reelection, by falsely delivering to the public that the unemployment rate dropped below 8 %.

The number of scandals the main stream media missed during his first term is appalling. I don't think you want to hear the litany

of them again, they run from Benghazi through NSA spying on the world. The liberal media hid the facts so they would not have legs, the very legs they are covering today, because they would look like fools if they didn't expose the obvious.

They didn't do their job then and the people are paying the price now for their lack of journalistic check and balance.

What a tiny web we weave when our intent is to deceive. I don't know who said it, but it seems to work.

CARNEY'S DAILY SITCOM . . . A C IS GOOD FOR OBAMACARE WEBSITE

Washington DC (Storch Report) November 18, 2013 -- It was the same old same old at Jay Carney's press gaggle today, more on the beleaguered website as though this was Obamacare's only problem.

No mention of the 5 million people that had their health insurance canceled, those that lost their doctors nor the extraordinary increase in premiums.

The same words continue to come out of Carney's mouth as though he departs the Oval office like a wind-up doll on replay.

There was a slight departure today, he said in effect the White House would be happy with a grade of C by December 1st. That's satisfying 8 out of 10 that go on the website. I guess that's better than their current success rate of 2 out of 10.

This White House sets their bar so low in their goals, by mid-December they might be touting a 20% failure rate.

Things are so bad, the President is telling the people by administrative directive they can go back to their subpar insurance if that's what they want and if they can find an insurance agency that will sell such a policy at an increase over what they were paying, but for one year.

"Hey, guys President Obama is shooting for a C by mid-December," Carney told the media with a smile.

"IT'S ON ME . . ." AND, "IT'S HUGE . . ."

Washington DC (Storch Report) November 14, 2013 -- President Obama held a press conference today telling us how he was going to fix Obamacare administratively, but refused to say that his signature legislation was broken, but nevertheless needed fixing, much like trying to put toothpaste back in the tube.

He said "no one informed him directly" that the website wasn't working. Does that mean he was told indirectly? Although he was in the dark, he said, "I feel deeply responsible."

With respect to his statement, "You can keep your plan," he tried to weasel out of it by saying that he thought the grandfather clause in the bill covered that, but, "it was an insufficient assumption. It's on me," he said. However he ignored the fact that he delivered this message to the people some 30 times and failed to admit that if he didn't continue to repeat this lie, the bill never would have passed.

Does this now mean you can send your health care bills to the White House because "It's on me," the president said?

I don't think so, because by executive order Obama once again violated the Constitution by directing insurance companies to reinstitute the old policies, five million of which have been cancelled, even though they do not meet the minimum requirements under the Affordable Care Act and the government would look the other way through 2014, the same action the president took with the mandate portion of the act.

There is no teeth in Obama's directive and following it could very well mean companies would be breaking the law.

Obama said during the Obamacare fixing press briefing that he, "fumbled the ball"... "And, should have done a better job." And, he promised to do a better job when he got the ball back.

But he has yet to recover the fumble, but in the meantime he is violating the Constitution by trying to bypass the law by executive order. It won't work, he can't put Humpty Dumpty back together again.

He did say he "should have done a better job." And he promised to do "a better job" when he got the ball back.

Obama admits that he has lost his credibility, "we fumbled the ball." And once again he said, "That's on me."

I would suggest Obama name Billy Fuccillo a Czar of credibility in the White House. Talk about a salesman, he's that King of Kia car sales with dealerships seemingly everywhere. His credibility far exceeds that of Obama's, he seems to give away as much as the president without using taxpayer's money, and his promises are HUGE from cruises, shopping sprees and iPads, and he does all of this without lying and sells cars at the same time.

OBAMA HEARING WHAH WHAH SOUNDS FROM GROWN-UPS IN DC

Washington DC (Storch Report) November 4, 2013 -- I think we put the wrong person in the White House two times around.

I don't want to get into the myriad of reasons I have discussed many times before for coming to this conclusion in the lead, I just want to focus on why President Obama thinks Washington is made up of grown-ups in Charlie Brown cartoons.

Today the president's spokesperson Jay Carney, White House Press Secretary, who has been under a lot of pressure lately, confirmed Obama's impression of adults in Washington comparing them to Charlie Brown's cartoons.

I guess Jay needed another metaphor to compare the GOP with, for I am sure that's who he was bashing, while once again fielding a barrage of questions on Obamacare trying to explain why it was working so well.

Jay may himself be living in cartoon land because he spins an Obamacare Charlie Brown yarn that could put a child to sleep during a bedtime story. And if this comparison doesn't work, he could always segue to Pinocchio.

He really believes the only problem with Obamacare is the website, although he did have a bit of a gaggle dealing with the White House Press corps explaining how the alternatives to going

through the website, allows the public options; however, all the information the public provides no matter the venue, still must go through the website portal, and it just doesn't work.

Otherwise, everything else is fine and the people love it, he says. You know, like you can keep your plan, Period; you can keep your doctor, Period. But hundreds of thousands can no longer find their plan nor their doctors and this has nothing to do with the website.

Any time someone from the Peanuts gang would chat with an adult, the response always sounded like, "Mwahmwahmwah, wah wah mwah." That's really the way Jay Carney sounded today and for the past week speaking on Obamacare. This is a classic Obama tactic to reverse a perceived accusation on his opponents.

Legendary comedian Jackie Mason said of Obama in a radio interview yesterday, "The whole country's walking around wondering if this guy's really the president of a country. He looks at you straight in the face, and tells you that if you want your plan, you got your plan, you keep your plan. Now, a month-and-a-half later, you got no plan, you lost your plan, and he tells you you still got a plan."

Apparently the best answer for Charlie Brown's trouble with adults talking so weird is that all kids hear is whah whah whah. Charlie Brown is in a kid's world and anything the grown-ups have to say isn't really relevant to him. A kid doesn't listen to what an adult says. All a kid hears is blah blah blah and that's what Obama is hearing according to Jay Carney.

Yup, we put a kid in the White House and that's all he is hearing, whah, whah. whah. Thanks for making it clear Charlie Brown.

WHAT IS IT THAT YOU DON'T UNDERSTAND?

Washington DC (Storch Report) November 2, 2013 -- Obama told you, you can keep your insurance. Period. You can keep your doctor. Period. Periods are important in sentences, they preclude qualifications. And he told you your insurance premiums will be lower.

I'll bet you misunderstood your president, he doesn't mislead, misspeak, utter falsehoods or lie despite being awarded four Pinocchio's by the Washington Post for telling a fib about Obamacare that made his nose grow a bit longer along with his ears that only hear what he wants them to.

You know after five years of extraordinary achievement on the economy, jobs, fast and furious, IRS targeting of conservatives, the FBI spying on journalists, Benghazi, and the NSA spying on the world, not to mention foreign affairs, there is just no room for duplicitousness in President Obama's soul.

You see what he said when he said it, he and his minions believe it to be true to this day.

Obama and his flunkies that speak for him are trumping up another falsehood worthy of a few more Pinocchio's by blaming the insurance companies for making a liar out of him on three counts.

He says, "Obamacare doesn't force you out of your plan. Your insurance company does."

This once again is untrue. The insurance companies are doing nothing but what you are trying to do, comply with the law. Obama knew he lied about these three compelling selling points of Obamacare in 2010 but continued to pitch them up to the present when he knew they were not true.

The insurance companies are complying with the law and they can only offer what the government tells them the minimum is that they can offer, which happens to be more than what they offered before at a lower price. For example they are required to provide maternity coverage for 55 year old men and women? Neither of which is of a child bearing age, that is if men ever were.

Obamacare law is the cause of the Obama lie and he knew it three years ago, but continued to sell the falsehood. This is precisely why polices have been canceled and premiums have in many cases doubled in cost.

President Obama, Jay Carney, White house press secretary and Valerie Jarrett, counsel to the President, should take their shtick on the road and recreate Abbott and Costello's, "Who's On First." vaudeville act and call it, "You can keep your insurance, Period." It would be just as understandable now as theirs was then.

IT'S HALLOWEEN AND COSTUME CORRECTNESS HAS REARED ITS SCARY FACE

Washington DC (Storch Report) October 25, 2013 -- It has finally happened, liberals are ruining Halloween for kids.

I never liked Halloween, I always thought I was begging for a treat by threatening a trick. I never knew a trick to threaten with, but we all said trick or treat.

Had I known what I was thinking then, I would have thought it was the beginning of wealth redistribution.

I mean after all the kids knew enough to go to the wealthy section of town, if you had one, I didn't, to threaten your treat or trick and to get your best reward.

In my day benefactors weren't putting razor blades in their treats, nor were kids exercising any tricks.

I mean after all, Halloween was conceived as a capitalist, commercial venture to sell costumes and candy, after all this is a big business for manufactures, dentists and doctors.

If I was a conservative, and knew what it meant, as Halloweener then, as I am now, as an anti-Halloweener adult, I would have recognized that this was a liberal wealth redistribution movement.

But now it has exponentially moved to another level of sophistication.

Now liberal universities, if there were the likes of any others in this nation, are telling their students that "certain Halloween costumes inappropriately perpetuate racial, cultural, and gender stereotypes."

This is going on at the University of Minnesota and the University of Colorado-Bolder.

The Dean of Students Christina Gonzales at the University of Colorado-Boulder said, "The CU-Boulder community has in the past witnessed and been impacted by people who dressed in costumes that included blackface or sombreros/serapes; people have also chosen costumes that portray particular cultural identities as overly sexualized, such as geishas, 'squaws,' or stereotypical, such as cowboys and Indians."

I want to tell you here and now, that if I met Pocahontas on my trails of trick and treating yesterday, I would have asked her out on a date.

What the hell, I never liked Halloween anyway.

SO, NOW I KNOW

Manasota Key FL (Storch Report) September 16, 2013 -- So, is the new starting point to a sentence, it is apparently the new 'in' word replacing, 'we', 'um,' 'like,' none of which serve much purpose of information and maybe that is the new intent of a conjunction.

Conjunction's now apparently give us time to think as to where we are going with our thoughts.

A conjunction is really supposed to serve to connect words, phrases, clauses or sentences.

We all like to be 'in' and to be 'in' with a new 'in' word like 'so.'

'So,' what is the word connecting with when you start the sentence with 'so?'

Nothing, I mean, it sounds like beginning a sentence with a non sequitur rather than ending a sentence with one, thus connecting a word like 'so' to nothing . . . anyway.

It sounds as though it would be a word Greg Gutfeld of Fox's The Five would ban, while tonight he served up a 'cull de sac of conjecture' to explain what no one seemed to know about the shootings today at the DC Navy Yard.

Perhaps reporters should have begun their reports with 'so,' it might have been more revealing.

We did, and 'so' perhaps we are 'in,' and we used the word correctly in this sentence. At least I think I did.

And if Gutfeld doesn't ban the word, I will, and never use it again to start a sentence.

Whatever . . .

MISSION OF FAILURE

Washington DC (Storch Report) September 14, 2013 -- We are just three years short of President Obama completing his mission of failure.

It will be then that we the people can take back and restore the course of the nation to what our founding fathers envisioned. We can leave Obama's legacy to the historians to sort out and they can be as flummoxed as he was in creating it.

I never thought a goal of failure would be something to reach for in life, but Obama has proven otherwise.

I guess if you are a progressive you want to take something that was 'exceptional' and make it less so leveling the playing field economically, militarily, racially, socially and financially, that is except for the 'exceptional' like the president and congress.

After all we live in a culture where political correctness declares even failures winners. We all get the equivalency of the Nobel Peace prize even if we don't deserve it.

That philosophically in itself is mind boggling for an American. But then again we might not be talking about an American philosophy, sounds and looks more European.

However, I do believe mentor Saul Alinsky would have been proud of Obama's leveling of the playing field, via his community organizing experience and degradation of a nation, even though

the people thought they were voting for something else. If you remember it was Joe the Plumber who really knew what was going on.

As a student of history I am appalled at what I'm witnessing, and disappointed in the voters of America that re-elected Obama to a second term after witnessing his poor performance during his first term. They should be kicking themselves in the ass for incompetence and a lack of common sense.

As I segue into senior citizenship and will have all the wonderful benefits of ObamaCare, such as dying sooner than later, I have come to the conclusion that the most important intellect that one can have is common sense.

Yes, I call common sense an intellect primarily because it can't be taught, you either have it or you don't. There are people with street smarts that have common sense and there are those with a Harvard education that are missing the common sense gene. President Obama happens to fall into this category, not even recognizing when he's in a chess game.

As Forest Gump said, "That's all I've got to say about that."

HEY ABBOTT

Washington DC (Storch Report) September 11, 2013 -- Comics, Abbott and Costello, the Three Stooges, and Stan & Ollie had more credibility in their day than President Obama's press secretary Jay Carney who is scrambling in his press briefings to defend the buffoonery of the administration he serves as spokesperson... and he does it all with a straight face.

It is, pardon the borrowing of a metaphor, a 'trickle down' effect of hypocrisy on just about every issue he must deal with and adapt to, the latest being Syria.

There should be empathy for Carney, for at this stage of both foreign and domestic relations over events in Syria, he would be better off representing President Vladimir Putin of Russia, as spokesperson.

It is almost as though we the people as well as the global community are asking, "Who's on first?"

Obama sends out his Secretary of State John Kerry to deliver a strong and forceful message about the president taking unilateral military action against Syria for using chemical weapons killing some 1400 of his own people, asks Kerry to defend his decision at hearings in congress, but then takes a walk in the Rose Garden with his Chief of Staff, Denis McDonough and a few days later asks for the sanction of war from congress.

There is little support for this action from the people or congress.

Obama then goes to the G20 in Russia fails to develop an international collation of support for military action against Syria.

Obama comes home and Putin executes a checkmate in what was a chess game Obama didn't know he was in and calls for Syria to turn over its chemical weapons of mass destruction and President Bashar Assad agrees. Obama tries to regroup and says he discussed this strategy with Putin, but there is no evidence of this political maneuver.

Obama then asks congress to delay its vote on military action, and it is then that one can hear a loud cry coming from Jay Carney's office at the White House, "Hey Abbott."

"THE RED LINE"

Washington DC (Storch Report) September 5, 2013 -- It was a few days before Labor Day that the White House discovered it had a crisis on its hands, it wasn't Fast and Furious, it wasn't Benghazi, it wasn't IRS targeting of conservatives, it wasn't the FBI spying on journalists or NSA spying on the world, these were already declared 'phony scandals,' it was, "The Red Line."

It was determined that it was once again time to consult with the spinmeisters from Chicago and call in the 'A Team.'

As a result former White House senior adviser and Obama campaign manager David Plouffe, former White House press secretary Robert Gibbs, former speechwriter Jon Favreau and former National Security Council spokesman Tommy Victor were convened to meet with President Obama over, 'The Red Line.'

According to the Wall Street Journal, Victor said the group was brought in to coordinate the administration's message on Syria. It was not exactly a barbecue party for the Labor Day weekend.

The subject was, 'The Red Line.' A debate ensued over the president drawing a line in the sand with respect to President Bashar Assad of Syria and his use of chemical weapons.

Thirteen months ago in the midst of a two year civil war in Syria, Obama said during a press briefing, "We have been very clear a 'red line' for us would be the movement of chemical weapons or the use of chemical weapons."

The group agreed that the objective should be to distance the president from this statement. One participant said, "but he said it . . . there's a video record." Another said so what, he has said a lot of things we have distanced himself from.

How about all the scandals we have deemed 'phony,' you don't see them in the news anymore? We should think about blaming it on someone else, and it was then that former President George W. Bush's name didn't escape consideration. "I think we have gone to that well once too often, how about 'humanity?'

'Humanity,' that's good said another, how about adding 'Congress and the international community?'

That's it, that's the message now we need to develop the strategy. Let's roll it out and deliver it through venues already in place, it was decided.

It was suggested they use House minority leader Nancy Pelosi to plant the seed of 'humanity' drawing the red line, not Obama. We can do this following the meeting at the White House with congressional leaders to discuss military action against Syria. It was then suggested as a follow up, that Secretary of State John Kerry clearly point out during his scheduled testimony before Congress on limited military action against Syria, that Obama didn't draw the red line, it was Congress and the international community that was originally against the use of chemical weapons during war.

And then to close the deal it was recommended that President Obama on his way to the G20 meeting in Russia, with a planned stop in Stockholm, say the following at a press briefing, "I did not set a red line, the Congress and the world set a red line," justifying the use of military action.

And, this is how George W. Bush escaped blame.

NO BOOTS ON THE GROUND, JUST ON THE PEOPLE'S DESK; A REWRITE OF THE 'RED LINE'

Washington DC (Storch Report) September 3, 2013 -- As we can see the boots are not on the ground, just a boot on the people's desk.

Act 2: Someone in the White House was working overtime this Labor Day weekend realizing that even a parent of a child knows that once you draw a 'red line' it must be challenged.

And so, it was decided President Obama, although he said it, didn't draw the 'red line,' it was humanity that did it.

The international community drew that line dating all the way back to WW I, when it was decided by the international community chemical weapons of mass destruction should not be used in war.

And, that's that, all that needs to be resolved now are boots on the ground v a boot on the people's desk. Very frankly I'm more concerned about Obama's foot on my desk. He has no respect for furniture that the people paid for. At least he could take his shoes off during a crisis.

And so today Congresswoman Nancy Pelosi was the first to announce at the White House following an Obama meeting on Syria that it was humanity that drew that 'red line' and then Secretary of State John Kerry reiterated the message later in the day before a Congressional hearing on Syria investigating the declaration of war.

Well that's not exactly the way Kerry tried to explain it, he says he knows war and that's not exactly what he's talking about.

It was Obama that drew the 'red line,' boxed himself between a rock and a hard place, or we wouldn't be in the midst of Congressional hearings discussing military action in Syria over the use of chemical weapons with no global or UN support and according to polls the people by a margin of 6 to 10 do not support unilateral military action.

Kerry said the cost of silence will have serious consequences; citing American's credibility and the message it will not only send to Syria and Assad, but to Iran and North Korea.

It is an interesting fact that 1,400 civilians were killed during Assad's chemical warfare attack two weeks ago including 426 children. Since the civil war broke out in Syria some 100,000 persons have been killed and Obama took no action. The calculus of the military strategy is to degrade, to deter, but not to destroy chemical weapons, nor to take part in a regime change. Kerry said Assad will survive the attack, to once again flaunt it, which says our Intel has no confidence at this stage in the rebels, which are apparently made up of Jihad Muslims.

There are no clear cut objectives by the administration, just a whim of no common sense policy; Kerry may have been in a war, but he has no understanding of the definition of one, for he described it today but didn't understand it was one; and it's obviously easier to recall a quote of a 'red line,' as he did, than it is a Tomahawk missile.

THE LINE OBAMA ONCE CALLED RED FADES TO GRAY

Washington DC (Storch Report) September 3, 2013 -- Are you confused, unclear, uncertain as President Obama appears to be over the 'proportional, limited, no boots on the ground, military action' against Syria over the use of gas killing 1,400 civilians, including 426 children, when Bashar Assad crossed Obama's proverbially Red Line by using Sarin gas?

That Red Line appears to be fading to Gray as Obama now says this military action in Syria is not 'Iraq or Afghanistan' and his Secretary of State John Kerry says it's about America's credibility and sending a message to Iran and North Korea while slapping the hand of a misbehaving child with Tomahawk missile strikes.

There is no announced end game, but Obama has made it clear this action is not about regime change, although he has made it clear Assad has to go.

First he sends Kerry out to sell war against Syria to the American people and to convince them Assad used gas and weapons of mass destruction against his own people with no indication he would take this war declaration to Congress for debate and approval.

Then days later after learning that America's closest ally, Great Britain's Parliament would not support military action against

Syria, Obama decides he would ask Congress for debate and congressional action, unlike his military attack on Libya.

Russia and China warn against war; the French are first supportive of the US with rhetoric then backs-off saying today that if the US Congress doesn't approve military action they are 'out,' and the UN warns the US against unilateral action.

Meanwhile as red fades to gray, the war element of surprise fades to confusion, the targets of a tailored action of war are being re-deployed by Assad and Obama is slipping into an abdication of leadership which may only be saved someday by a teleprompter's rhetoric.

Columnist Charles Krauthammer summed it all up in two words: "Amateur Hour."

AND, IF IT WASN'T FOR SNOWDEN WE WOULDN'T KNOW THE GOVERNMENT IS SPYING ON US . . .

Washington DC (Storch Report) August 17, 2013 -- President Obama would tell us if he was snooping on us? He wouldn't tell us something else to make us believe in him, would he? You know, because it's a violation of the Fourth Amendment to the Constitution to snoop on the people? You can believe that what he says about this subject is true because he taught constitutional law? I mean he wouldn't lie to the people he serves?

But why does it feel like, Edward Snowden, a fugitive from justice living in asylum in Russia is telling the truth and the president of the United States is lying to me?

I mean, after all this is not a good feeling, but as the facts unfold why is Snowden beginning to look like a hero and Obama like a bum?

As a backdrop, why does the Obama administration cover-up Fast & Furious, Benghazi, FBI spying on journalists including the AP, Fox's James Rosen, the IRS targeting and intimidating conservative groups and the National Security Agency (NSA) literally spying on the world including US citizens, and then paint them as scandals and have President Obama call them unfounded and trumped up by Republicans trying to block his policies?

The main stream media does its best to protect its rights under the First Amendment, but seemed to do little to protect its rights under the constitution, when the FBI was spying on their journalists and furthermore relied on Snowden, a former systems analyst and whistleblower with NSA, to uncover the government's spying on the people of the United States, and for that matter, the rest of the world.

The Washington Post unveiled a few days ago through an internal NAS audit and other top-secret documents from Snowden that the agency has broken privacy rules or overstepped its legal authority thousands of times each year since Congress granted the agency broad new powers in 2008.

Yet only a few days before Obama went on vacation he told the people otherwise at a White House press briefing.

In an unrelated 'Green" issue of policy, Obama is having another Solyndra solar moment and having panels installed on the roof top of the White House in spite of the people's or Congresses wishes. They call it a bypass, it is popular for the heart and within the Obama administration.

Perhaps it is because we are but the green geckos of the world just feeling blue over the degree of Obama's scandalous mendacity.

IT IS WHAT IT IS . . .

Manasota Key FL (Storch Report) Aug 11, 2013 -- Is the cliché, "It is what it is as stupid as it sounds?

If it is, why is it used so often?

Most cliché's are trite and reflect a negative, but unanimous consensus that says we can't do anything about a situation that is what it is.

And so we throw up our hands and all agree that we have to put up with whatever we are talking about and there seems to be more of these situations day by day.

Cliché's have been around for a long time, they just seem to change with the generations of the times and the latest stays in vogue until the next comes along.

For example there once was, "Qu Sera, Sera (Whatever will be will be . . .) that Doris Day made into a song and everybody bought into, for whatever reason.

Then there was, "That's the name of the game," and for some reason whatever the situation was we labeled it with that cliché and did nothing about whatever it was we should have done something about.

And the shortest one-word cliché was, "Whatever" . . . It seems to me to be much like the Japanese waving the white flag during World War II in the Pacific and saying "No Mas." Well, I guess they didn't say that, but I know they waved the white flag.

Why these negative cliché's, take on a negative connotation that we readily buy into and do nothing about?

In 2012 the nation bought into Obama as a second term president when we could have done something about him based upon his first term of lackluster performance, and did nothing, and now we say, "It is what it is."

During his first term he rammed through Obamacare with a Dem controlled Senate and House, and now we say, "It is what it is," and do nothing.

And yesterday, Bo, the first dog flew on his own plane to The Vineyard to be with the First Family on vacation. I guess he's not welcome on Air Force One. Could this be dog racism, or just, "It is what it is . . .?"

Is this Phenom a crowd mentality where it is easier to buy into what it is, rather than do something about what it should be, because it's easier to accept what it is realizing that you can't do anything about it after all?

OBAMA: 'I DID THE DISHES'

Washington DC (Storch Report) Aug 9, 2013 -- President Obama tried using a metaphor to launch his trust-building initiative as a result of Edward Snowden's leaks on NSA spying on the world by comparing it to convincing Michelle that he 'washed the dishes' . . . and it wasn't any more believable than we the people believing that the government hasn't and isn't spying on us and the rest of the world.

Imagine the conversation between Barack and Michelle over the dish washing metaphor.

"Honey I did the dishes."

"I don't believe it Barack."

"Come here I'll show you."

"How will I know you did them?"

"Well, they're clean."

"But, how can I believe you did them, just because you said you did them."

"Well honey, let me think about that, because I want to instill trust between us so that when I say I did the dishes you will believe me."

"Allow me to discuss this with my staff and I will get back to you with a trust-building initiative on dish washing."

A few nights later at dinner Obama unveiled his four point program on building trust with Michelle in his dish washing initiative.

"Honey, I have asked the FBI to take my fingerprints so that anytime you have a question about who did the dishes we can have the plates dusted to determine whose prints were last on the plates."

"Secondly, I am going to be more transparent about my dish washing and do it when you and the kids can see it."

"I also thought I would get a digital copy of my dish washing off the internal security system and post it on YouTube."

"And lastly, I have appointed an oversight committee to prepare a preliminary report for you within 60 days and a final one by year-end on the dish washing trust-initiative."

"Barack you are talking to me, your wife. Trust between us is not something you build through and initiative of third party documentation and rhetoric, it is built through character and knowing when you can trust that one is telling the truth."

"Tell it to the people, perhaps they will believe you are doing the dishes, they have bought everything else you have said so far."

Meanwhile somewhere in Russia Edward Snowden is smiling as he and Putin are clinking their shot glasses of Vodka

WHEN LESS OF LIFE FACES YOU

Manasota Key FL (Storch Report) July 6, 2013 -- Growing old is big business for the young, perhaps one of the better investments in today's faltering economy, because the elderly need care.

After all everyone is living longer these days and the longer we live, we exponentially gather infirmities.

I recently had the opportunity to visit a few high end, end of life facilities, where people go to live out their waning years in style.

These facilities are much like a five star hotel where the staff is paid well to be nice, much like the staff of the Plaza Hotel in New York, or an exclusive country club.

The buildings on land are as graceful as cruise ships at sea.

There are hall-way get-together parties weekly, much like they have on cruise ships, nightly movies in a theater with no steps, preceded by dinner in elegant dining rooms where you dress in your finery, as you walk your walkers to your table, and pass a bevy range of parked Rolls Royce's to Chevy walkers.

There are opportunities to be active every moment of the day, for the social entertainment director makes you feel wanted and taking a nap in your luxury condo style apartment makes you feel as though you will be missed.

Your refrigerator freezer is filled with left-over doggie bags of food for snacks from the previous night's dinner in the posh dining rooms.

Jitney's shuttle you from place to place with storage for your walkers.

If you want to take your dog with you for breakfast or lunch, you can dine outside with a bark or two.

All the amenities are available, golf, tennis, cards, croquet, lectures, courses, a library, physical fitness rooms and it is all up to you and your ability to execute what you are capable of, or not.

And if not does take place, there is another section of these high end facilities for you to go to before the final resting place.

In many respects it is reminiscent of the film comedy "Defending Your Life" with Albert Brooks and Meryl Streep where they both fall in love with each other in a science fiction passage after death and they are in an interim state where they must prove themselves before a jury in order to move on, or return to earth.

Streep is in a posh hotel and Brooks is in the equivalent of Motel 7 where you have to turn out the lights when you leave. All can eat all they want. It is much like these high end phase-out facilities, jitneys take you everywhere, there is much to do, but it is a passage to somewhere else. Streep moves on, Brooks is sent back to earth, but before both depart love wins out in this Hollywood performance and they both move on.

I think I would like to stay in place until the final passage fades to dark.

I WONDER IF WE COULD GET A PARDON FOR MICHELE AND PRESIDENT OBAMA

Washington DC (Storch Report) July 2, 2013 -- While traveling throughout Africa on an estimated $100 million boondoggle with President Obama and her extended family, the First Lady, Michelle Obama, described living in the White House as like being in a "really nice prison."

Michelle's comment came during her discussion with former First Lady Laura Bush today at the African First Ladies Summit in Tanzania during an interview moderated by ABC journalist Cokie Roberts.

Roberts mentioned that Martha Washington, also described living in the role as First Lady, akin to being a state prisoner.

Michelle said she loved her job and found it liberating in some respects, but confining in others.

"There are some prison elements to it," she allegedly joked. "But it's a really nice prison."

Former first lady Laura Bush told the crowd that First Ladies had their own chef.

"You can't complain," Michelle admitted. "But there is definitely elements that are confining."

The White House is so confining to Michelle that she is wrapping-up an African swing of nations with her husband and family

to South Africa, Senegal and Tanzania. The first family cut back on a safari tour that would have required the expense of a sharp-shooting team to protect them against wild animals. Naturally the $100 million travel expense on taxpayer money sparked criticism as the federal government is dealing with its sequester-related budget cuts.

The Obamas are accompanied by hundreds of Secret Service agents and staff. Military cargo planes brought 56 vehicles including 14 limousines and three trucks loaded with bulletproof glass to cover the windows of the hotels where the Obamas stayed. And, fighter jets flew in the air space above the first family to provide round the clock protection.

"For the cost of this trip to Africa, you could have 1,350 weeks of White House tours, "Rep George Holding (R-NC) said on the House floor last week. White House tours have been canceled due to sequester-related budget cuts, a budget cut President Obama suggested and selected to cut White House tours.

I wonder if there is some way we the people can grant a pardon to First Lady Michelle Obama and her husband President Obama from the prison called the White House that they are so unjustly confined to.

DIPLOMACY AT G8: OBAMA & PUTIN TUSSLE OVER USE OF GYM, SYRIA

Dublin Ire (Storch Report) June 19, 2013 -- There was no meeting of the minds between President Obama and President Vladimir Putin at the G8 Summit in Dublin, they didn't agree on Syria, it was a chilly photo op and then Putin went for a chilly swim in a nearby lake all over a scheduling dispute over a fitness gym at the hotel both were staying at.

It took a while for the story to unfold, so we really don't know who did what when..

Nevertheless there appears to be a chill in the air between Russia and the United States over Syria and the US decision to supply rebel forces with weapons and Putin's comments, "Our opinions do not coincide." he said. "But all of us have the intention to stop the violence in Syria," Obama echoed.

But it was the gym scheduling that seemed to make more news, you see boys will be boys, even when dealing with diplomacy on a global basis. There seemed to be something macho being demonstrated.

Obama operatives apparently scheduled the gym first, and it could have been a laughable sticking point in the talks. Instead of the two world leaders agreeing to share the gym, some news reports said Putin backed down, and while Obama worked out in

air-conditioned comfort, the notoriously tough Putin went for a swim in a nearby lake.

In Chess parlance it might have been called a Macho Checkmate.

World leaders with nuclear power acting like children in a sandbox.

SCOOPERS V SODA JERKS, A JOB NOT SO EASY TO QUALIFY FOR TODAY

Irvington NJ (Storch Report) June 9, 2013 -- When I was a kid one of the part time jobs I always wanted was to be a Soda Jerk.

I accomplished that childhood dream and worked at three soda fountains in those formative years and at one of them followed in the footsteps of the comic Jerry Lewis at Gerstein's Drug Store on the corner of Union Place and Chancellor Avenue in Irvington, New Jersey.

At the time I really didn't realize how politically incorrect the title Soda Jerk was, that is until now when researching the mixology of ice cream, soda, seltzer, chocolate syrup and now they have added yogurt and coffee laden caffeine to what once was called an ice cream parlor.

I guess it really isn't politically correct today to have Jerk in any title of any job, even though it had a significant meaning then. You see it came from that jerky movement that the kid behind the counter used to squirt the seltzer into the drink coming from those fancy knobs that were featured at every soda fountain.

And to qualify to be a jerk to pull those fancy knobs was not as complex as it is today and when you think of what you were being called, it is no wonder in retrospect that they changed the name of the server.

But it was looked upon affectionately, we were serving something that is still being enjoyed today despite our politically correct choices of what is called healthy food.

My job of yesterday as a Soda Jerk is now called a Scooper.

No not a snooper, that's another story.

I really don't know if today I would dream of being a Scooper, I liked the Soda Jerk of yesterday, it was somewhat romantic, I mean look at the picture at the top of this column.

Today we have 7.6% unemployment with some 4 million people without jobs, so it is probably more difficult tor a teenager to get a job today than it was in my day, but perhaps our egos were not as large nor was the minimum wage at $8 per hour as it is today.

And so I looked into what it takes to be a scooper today.

What I found in one ice cream & frozen yogurt shop was what appeared to be a contract between the employee, who was identified as a "kid" and the parent, both of which had to sign what looked like an agreement to me.

The document was labeled, "Ice Cream & Frozen Yogurt Employee Orientation & Understanding."

The store said in its opening remarks. it was, "always looking for smart hard-working and personable kids. We have had great success over the years with our scoopers based upon the glowing feedback we get from our customers. And, our scoopers have learned many valuable life skills from working in our fast-paced environment."

They went on to say in this document that the "kid" had to have a 2.5 GPA or higher, the physical ability to do the work required, such as leaning over, scooping hard ice cream, carrying boxes and/or ice cream barrels up or down stairs and have a friendly outgoing nature and speak English.

They then outlined the work schedule in detail. During the summer months, mid-June through Labor Day the kids should be available 15-30 hours a week and during the Spring and Fall school year 10 to 15 hours per week.

Kids then had to provide bank account information to enable direct deposit of pay checks, follow-up with school and parents to determine working paper requirements and then both the kid and their parents had to sign the document.

I don't know if Jerry Lewis or I would have made it today as a scooper, after all we were just soda jerks.

THE COLOR OF BASKETBALL

Manasota Key Fl (Storch Report) April 6, 2013 -- I watched the last two college basketball teams in the final four last night and what I saw was the iridescent color of orange and that was team Syracuse and the iridescent color of yellow and that was team Michigan, skinny players flopping around in over-sized Bermuda shorts and shirts of cut-off sleeves and for the most part black legs and shaved black heads and thought to myself, this is the rainbow colors of basketball today.

I'm getting to the point that I'm rooting for the team with the color I like.

I already know I'm for the black team running up and down the court in those iridescent uniforms, because for the most part I don't see many white players on the court. I mean, I know that I've been brain washed to believe that white men can't jump, they can't run and they are short, so there's not too many white men that make the team.

It's almost like basketball has become what the old Negro baseball league was.

Now I like basketball, I once played it in college, and when I watch it today I like to root for a team and I find myself in a quandary. I'm already rooting for the black players and if I don't have a favorite team, all I have left is to pick the team with the color uniforms that I like. And I don't like how sloppy they look.

Oh, and the narrators of the game, they get so excited today even in a non-excitable game, I think they have ADHD and I'm ready to call 911, or prescribe Ritalin.

Even at half time the color commentators are so exuberant, and I don't know if it's over the resilient colors of the rainbow, or the game, that I too have to search for an extra antihypertensive.

Oh, by the way the iridescent yellow team won, it was the one I was rooting for. They are going to play the black team in white uniforms that won the previous game.

The colors of the final on Monday, Louisville in iridescent white on black and Michigan in iridescent yellow on black. I'm wearing my Ray-Bans to watch this one.

OBAMA'S MEANING OF CHANGE REVEALED

Washington DC (Storch Report) March 30, 2013 The inner premise and thought process of the Obama Manifesto goes something like this:

If Obama can build support from Hispanics through immigration reform, amnesty for illegals; legalize same sex marriage for gays; food stamps for the alleged poor; gun control for those opposed to the 2nd amendment of the constitution; and carbon emission controls through executive order calling for higher gas taxes for the pollution and climate warming freaks; he will have the demographic votes to recapture the house in 2014, and will have the majority of the population beholden to entitlements, big government and a new world order of Marxism.

This along with a few other tweaks during his remaining two years in office with total control of both houses should provide him with his legacy and transition him to his next power play.

With his signature legislation of costly Obamacare, the $17 trillion deficit he dramatically contributed to in a short four years, the 78% increase in the use of food stamps he created since being in office – putting some 48 million households on this entitlement, all of which are enjoying the cash flow at casinos, cruise ships and posh vacation spots – he will have put the final nail in the coffin of

a nation we once knew, all through the tactic of community organization. And, a nation once hooked on entitlements will be addicted to the dole forever.

And with the armed Brown Shirts he can maintain liberal control of the population with his brain washed Militia.

This then should play well into the new global order with the financial collapse of the rest of the world he can conveniently segue from the White House at the end of his presidential term, to become global President of the United Nations.

By then, as he will have accomplished individual and global wealth redistribution and put the United States on equal footing with the rest of the world, he can be King as Alinsky envisioned for him in "Rules for Radicals."

RE-BRANDING THE PAPACY FOR THE 21ST CENTURY

Rome (Storch Report) March 15, 2013 -- It all began on the 13th of March in the year 2013 when a humble man from Argentina was named Papa, much like Hemingway and not dissimilar to me who is known to his grandchildren as Pop Pop.

It just got me to thinking as to how much the Catholic Church needs some re-branding for the 21st century.

I mean, take it from me who was baptized a Lutheran, confirmed a First Reformed, with Sunday school medals reaching from my chest to my waist, married the first time in a Presbyterian Church, in between went to a Southern Baptist Church, and got married the second time in an Episcopal Church and since have only entered any domination of a church for weddings and funerals.

I have only observed Cardinal Jorge Mario Bergoglio, now with a new name he selected, except for the title he was elected to, Pope Francis, for a day-and-a-half.

The evening of his first appearance on the Vatican balcony, one he will appear on many times for the rest of his life, he asked for silence, bowed, and asked the throngs in St. Peter's Square to pray for him.

And, from that moment, perhaps to ever be, he was labeled the Pope of Humility. The symbol portrayed was simple. But it was profoundly broadcast as a moving image by his minions.

The following morning, as the media reported it, he 'slipped' out, as though the Pope could slip out of his red slippers without anyone noticing, of the Vatican in a black limo and went to the hotel where he was staying before sequestration to vote for a Pope that was to be him, to pick up his luggage, pay his bill – not exactly the same sequestration that President Obama was going through in the US – and then go to a Rome Jesuit Church to pray with the people.

It was then through symbolism that to me he was deemed through Devine intervention the Pope of Humility.

Think about it, he could have sent the limo to pick up his luggage, pay the hotel bill and pray at the Vatican, where more prayers are delivered perhaps per minute than any other place in the world.

But no, he wanted to pray with the people, he wants to pay for his own hotel bill, pick up his own bags, live in a small apartment, and ride the subway as he did in Buenos Aires.

I can't help but wonder whether the Vatican gives him his own AMEX card labeled Pope Francis?

After reviewing this brief bio of a man I haven't heard of before, I couldn't help but wonder about the re-branding of the Papacy for the 21st century and whether Pope Francis isn't the intellectual, but down to earth simple man to pull it all off?

Allow me to tell you why Pope Francis might just be the man to transform the church into the 21st century.

Following my days of being a cynical journalist, I went into the field of imagery – it's called public relations – for which I was equally cynical.

But do not doubt my qualifications to help the Catholic Church, despite my lack of knowledge of its religious heritage. You see in the field of propaganda, a word the Catholic Church coined, you don't let the facts get in the way of a good story. The Bible never did, nor did those that propagandized it over the years.

It is here that we need a bit of background for me to convince you of my message.

There are 1.2 billion Catholics in the world, and statistically the flock is decreasing. That is not a good thing and the Vatican is concerned about it along with the financial scandals it must deal with at the Vatican Bank and the ongoing Pedi file cases among the priests that do not seem to go away.

Now I know the church doesn't like me talking about this, but I'm trying to serve up the big idea Papacy, so bear with me.

Among the 1.2 billion Catholics worldwide, more than 40% of them come from Latin America. I'm sure this didn't go un noticed among the Cardinals voting to send up white smoke for Jorge.

After all we need more of a flock not a Fluke, from the US to seek free contraceptives for sex three times a day.

My first recommendation is that every time Pope Francis presents himself on the balcony in St. Peter's square or on a global stage, the song, "Don't Cry for Me Argentina" by Madonna be blasted out on the speakers to the roar of the followers. It would be much like the New York Yankees playing New York New York at the end of their games.

A concert should be held in St. Peter's Square by Madonna in Vatican robes, a striking juxtaposition, and both good for the Church and Madonna.

The Pope should then take her on a worldwide tour. The people will love it, especially in Latin America.

Use the film Evita for background symbolism.

I would suggest the Vatican consult with Notre Dame, an institution of higher learning in the US, which has developed a love hate relationship with a multitude of fans to see how well this is working for them and how the Vatican can apply this strategy.

Cheer leaders should be hired to be used as an advance team prior to Papal Pope visits. Imagine cheers for 'The Pope of the People', or 'The Pope of Humility,' or give me a 'P' an 'O' a 'P' and an 'E'.

All of this is but a diversionary tactic that I stole from President Obama, for the Catholic Church, until it can get its act together and join the 21st century. It is a time for transformation, not transparency.

Just a thought out of the box, the Deity made me do it.

As the Pope said, 'Buenos Aires'!

WE SHOULD CHOOSE A PRESIDENT THE WAY CATHOLICS CHOOSE A POPE

Washington DC (Storch Report) March 13, 2013 -- If we in the United States elected a president the way Catholics select a Pope we would significantly reduce a major financial burden on our nation and discover the solution to most of our problems.

It would probably cost a few bucks to build something like the Sistine Chapel and find someone like Michelangelo to do the painting, but in the very short term we would have a return on our investment. We would use it once every four years to elect a president and do so digitally rather than through a smoke stack and in-between election years we would charge for tours.

Prayer would have to be invoked into the system, and as we have found out from recent events we need a lot more of that.

We would have to deal with the ACLU, but we have been through that before. Imagine bringing prayer back into our school system, we might even resolve the gun issue.

But allow me to get to the big idea.

By adopting a system of Cardinals, we could call them something else, like Czars; the deity would then seek divine intervention. We could use a little of that.

This would result in no longer having to write welfare checks.

We wouldn't have to provide free cell phones or free internet.

There would be no more cash for clunkers or provide food stamps.

Section 8 housing would be eliminated and we could get rid of Sandra Fluke's free contraceptives and sex three times a day.

Medicaid would go and 99 weeks of unemployment would be eliminated. People would have jobs.

There would be no more free medicine and we would return capitalism to its rightful place.

All of this would thus be the solution to our current problems, the deficit would disappear and we would have a balanced budget; the major problem would be eliminated – there would no longer be a need for Democrats, there voting for these entitlements and doing so long after they are gone.

Just a thought!

NA NA NA NA NA; I DISCUSSED IT WITH MICHELLE, WE'RE CLOSING THE WHITE HOUSE TO TOURS

Washington DC (Storch Report) March 5, 2013 -- Barack: Michelle, I'm thinking about closing the White House to tours over sequestration, what you think"

Michelle: Right on Barack, I'm tired of the people thinking that this is their house and traipsing through it. This is our house and we proved it during the last election. How much do you think we can save?

Barack: Oh, not much. The people only tour the East Wing and they are self-guided tours. It's the principle of the whole sequestration issue. I was embarrassed by it all. You know it was my idea. It's the only bi-partisan bill I was able to really get through in my first term. If I can't say the janitors are going to lose their jobs in the Capitol and be right, I'm going to close the White House to tours, because I can and be right about something.

Michelle: You tell em' Barackie. I'm with you, this will give me time to deal with my new doggie diet initiative in telling families how to feed their dogs. I'm thinking of calling Mayor Bloomberg of New York to schedule an expensive lunch up there with him to discuss how we can collaborate to mutually ban more things that

we enjoy that we think the common man shouldn't have because it's bad for them.

Barack: That's brilliant Michelle that should prove to be an excellent distraction to the negative. You know, I've taken a terrible hit in the polls on this sequestration issue.

Michelle: I wouldn't worry too much about it, after all you are the Teflon president of all time, and this too shall pass.

GOP ONLY NEEDS $500,000 TO GET SOME FACE TIME WITH OBAMA

Chicago IL (Storch Report) February 26, 2013 -- It's all about the money. Hollywood knows how to deliver, the GOP doesn't.

All John Boehner, Speaker of the House has to do is pony up $500,000 to Obama's Organization for Action (OFA), formerly known as Organizing For America, which was the name for Obama's reelection campaign in 2012 and his election campaign in 2008.

The Chicago-based office never shut down even though Obama became a lame duck president winning his second term, it just modified its name, maintaining its acronym and changing Organizing to Organization and America to Action.

And instead of it functioning as a campaign office to re-elect a president it is now a public relations tax exempt community organization campaigning for Obama's radical social welfare policies on a grass roots level.

Now the GOP could get in the game if it would just learn to cooperate, compromise and kick in $500,000 a year and it would be guaranteed at least four face time meetings a year with Obama and the nation wouldn't be constantly pestered with gridlock, sequestration and budgets.

After all what is a mere $500,000 from the GOP coffers, when dealing with a $17 trillion deficit? This way everybody could

once again belong to the beltway club and enjoy the cronyism of yesterday.

Between the acronyms of OFA and MSNBC, where David Axelrod and Robert Gibbs now reside, making the network a bona fide propaganda arm of the State, allows Obama to cement into history his legacy of radical left wing social welfare policies.

C'mon John get in the game . . . ya gotta pay to play!

THE TRANSPARENCY WE CAN DO WITHOUT

Manasota Key Fl (Storch Report) February 21, 2013 -- It seems we always get the transparency we don't need to know and that which we seek from our government we can't have.

A group of New Zealand physicians have determined it's not only OK, but preferred, that passengers pass gas mid-flight.

Anecdotal evidence shows that flying increases one's likelihood of passing gas, a natural phenomenon that happens 10 times per day.

And when you hold it in there are significant drawbacks for the individual, such as discomfort, pain, bloating dyspepsia (indigestion), pyros is (heartburn) just to name a few resulting in abdominal symptoms.

However, this article found that there was a time when you shouldn't pass gas in flight, and that is when you are a member of the cock pit crew.

WHAT KIND OF A GUN TO BUY? BIDEN RECOMMENDS A SHOTGUN

Uncle Joe Biden our Vice President, who more often than not puts his foot in his mouth and who the president put in charge of his proposals banning the sale of assault weapons and to spearhead the promotion of Obama's proposals battling gun violence, recommends people buy a shotgun.

"Guess what," Biden said, "a shotgun will keep you a lot safer, a double barreled shotgun, than the assault weapon in somebody's hands (who) doesn't know how to use it, even one who does know how to use it," the outspoken veep, a shot gun owner himself, replied to a question. "It's harder to use an assault weapon to hit something than it is a shotgun."

"You want to keep people away in an earthquake? Buy some shotgun shells."

Earthquake, shells? I don't know where the earthquake came from and what you do with the shells if you don't have a gun, but that's Uncle Joe.

I guess he often finds himself speaking out of both ends of the human anatomy when walking the fine line in behalf of the administration when speaking of the second amendment. Perhaps he should take a flight.

Whatever . . .

PERSONHOOD

Washington DC (Storch Report) February 16, 2013 -- There was a day when a person wore a chip on their shoulder and a hair shirt too, but in today's culture of heightened sensitivity if one is not careful with their words one could lose their job. Is it any wonder that unemployment is pushing 8 percent?

There also was a time when corporations used to hold classes in sensitivity training for their executives, but that seemed to fall out of vogue as they began to lose too many employees to a heightened level of sensitivity.

I grew up in a middle class blue collar multi-ethnic community where everyone called each other by a slang term other than the accepted ethnicity of their origin, but they too wore hair shirts and what today is termed politically incorrect was looked upon then as an affectionate term.

There were polish kids that were known as Polak instead of being called by their given first name. They even signed their year books as such.

It was a day when people knew who they were and what role to play. It was a day when he was a he and she was a she and didn't try to be a him.

It was a day when boys went out with girls and girls went out with boys and a matinee was going to the movie or for an ice cream sundae at the local soda shop and condoms weren't

handed out through a government entitlement program in the 6th grade.

Oh, and it was a day when marriage was between a man and a woman and the woman didn't want to be the man and the man never wanted to be the woman.

Then the day came when woman wanted what man had and equal opportunity reared its political correctness across all races and genders within our culture and what was once perceived as a complement became a sexist politically incorrect statement.

Even Mayor Bloomberg of New York, who tries to do all the right things by his Manhattanites by banning cigarettes, salt, big soda and now Styrofoam coffee cups, stepped out of line when admiring a woman's ass at a cocktail party and was labeled a sexist.

When I was in the military gays were banned, but if they somehow slipped by, and later found out, they were thrown out. Then the time came for don't ask don't tell and even then they could tell even though they didn't ask and were still thrown out.

But the day came under the Obama administration when gays were welcomed in the military and right around the corner looms same sex marriage and women fighting on the front lines in our country's wars. Now that's what I call real equal opportunity.

When two gay women marry where they legally can like California, one usually refers to the other as 'my wife,' but you never hear the wife refer to the other as 'my husband'. I guess in this case she doesn't want to be her or whatever role she is playing. I wonder who takes out the garbage.

What was right is now wrong and what was wrong is now right.

Think about it, today we have a black man living in a white house who is a champion of the middle class. He wants to take money from the rich, who worked there ass off to build what he says they didn't, and give it to the middle class. Where was he when I was growing up?

This is the same guy who on Valentine's Day took his wife Michelle to an upscale restaurant in DC, where most couldn't get a reservation in a lifetime. You see this joint only has 12 seats, and he got a table for two on the spur of the moment. The tab for the evening with wine was more than $900 for two, which comes down to about $10 a bite.

This all was most likely coming off while middle class Valentine couples were munching on a horse meat burger at the local fast food joint for less than a $1 a patty; or they could have done Chinese at what is now known as a pan-Asian restaurant. I'll bet they still have columns A & B on the menu.

Political correctness appears to be a perception thing. And this perception is determined by the power brokers of our culture. And there is no higher broker than the occupant of the White House.

It is traditional following the President's State of the Union address for networks to give rebuttal time to the opposing party. And so this time the Republicans picked its rising star Sen. Marco Rubio of Florida to give the address. All was going well in refuting Obama's remarks until he decided he needed a drink of water.

That's right water, something all speakers, politicians and athletes partake in. But you see Rubio awkwardly reached for the bottle of water took a swig and there was the opportunity Obama's public relations arm in Chicago was looking for. There motto is never let a good crisis go to waste.

They saw this as the perfect opportunity to distract from Rubio's message and billed him as being nervous and suffering from dry mouth. The left wing media, another extension of the administration, picked up the story and aired it hundreds of times.

It was a classic example of taking something that was politically correct to do and turn it into a perception of incorrectness to divert attention from the message.

The following day they did it once again at the President's prayer breakfast where Dr. Benjamin Carson, a renowned pediatric neurosurgeon at Johns Hopkins lectured Obama on his failed policies of his first term in office. Albeit couched in religious terms, the speech was cast as being politically incorrect by the administration.

We live in a highly sensitive culture today where it seems to be appropriate to apologize at the outset for what we might likely say because it is sure to offend someone.

That is precisely why I was so careful to pick the title for this column. You see, it's not ethnic, sexiest, or racist and is gender neutral. But, I'll bet I offended the hoods in Chicago.

Whatever . . .

TACO BELL CASTS-OFF THE ELDERLY IN SUPER BOWL AD

Manasota Key FL (Storch Report) February 4, 2013 -- I guess the demographic audience for Taco Bell products tails off after the age of 50, that's when you're eligible for membership in AARP and the return to the bottom line for Taco products apparently diminishes the older a person gets so it appears that the geezer is fair game to make fun of when they are no longer useful to the corporation's profits.

This is the image Taco Bell projected in its Super Bowl commercial, copying a scene from the movie Cocoon to portray senior citizen behavior, but the flick was funny and in good taste, the Taco Bell ad was not.

It was insulting, degrading and disgraceful to our senior citizens suggesting a lack of respect and ignoring the inevitable the copy writers who prepared this script might face if they are fortunate to make it to the age of the people they were glibly making sick fun of.

It apparently appealed to the young when it was mocking senior citizens who were probably asleep at the time the commercial aired.

In this ad a group of young-at-heart grandpas and grannies sneak out of a nursing home for a night of reveling, getting tattoos

on their back, appearing bombed on the top of cars in costumes, carousing in swimming pools, acting like children partying hard and fast like a bunch of mischief-makers before ending the night at — where else? — Taco Bell.

This ad would never run in Japan, where the nation reveres and respects the elderly, rather than making fun of their infirmities.

Instead of knocking the elderly that Taco Bell has apparently written-off and is disrespectful of, imagine the opportunity they are missing by not appealing to the senior citizen's love of hot spicy food slipping through our porous borders from Mexico and doing a cooperative marketing effort with the manufactures of the purple pill Nexium suggesting those over 50 take one before visiting Taco with the assurance of free after dinner mints of Tums to avoid esophageal reflux.

Another idea might be for Taco to introduce soft chips for the elderly to prevent broken dentures.

And lastly Taco might consider recommending seniors take a dose of Imodium before tucking back in at the nursing home after a night of partying to prevent Montezuma Revenge.

I guess the days of attacking penguins and mocking dwarfs from being used as bowling balls are over and it is now fair game on the elderly. So much for the growing trend of political correctness.

WHO SHRUNK THE ECONOMY?

Washington DC (Storch Report) January 30, 2013 -- It was the 'predecessor' that shrunk the economy said Jay Carney, White House Press Secretary, who apparently couldn't remember the name of the previous, President, George W. Bush, today because it was so long ago.

Other Dem's blamed the Republicans, another generic reference without name calling, perhaps Bush bashing in Obama's second term is being softened.

But you can count on 'bashing' not escaping the Obama vernacular during his to-be-eight year political campaign on issues he takes to the people to pressure congress to submit to his conquests rather than governing through leadership and compromise. I think it's called a 'dictatorship.'

Issues that are now on his plate such as immigration reform, which he wants now; gun control, which he wants now; and bashing Fox News and Rush Limbaugh because they don't say what he likes, are high on his agenda.

He went to Las Vegas to sell immigration reform, even though there was a bi-partisan deal on the table before he left, at a taxpayer cost of $1.8 million and now he is off to Minneapolis Thursday to sell gun control.

Obama doesn't seem to like to deal with his colleagues in congress – he is a lonely man in the White House who likes to go to

Camp David and skeet shoot with friends, which we only learned of recently.

I guess this helps with not trying to change the constitution.

Obama is a master magician, constantly taking the people's eye off the trick through distractions to create the magic.

Rahman Emanuel, the Mayor of that Chicago town, that has more deaths by guns than has occurred in Afghanistan, advised Obama to never let a good crisis go to waste, and he hasn't.

Obama is always on the offense, effectively using the tactic of divide and conquer, a Saul Alinsky disciple, a community organizer that works on dumbing down the community he is selling and organizing for his objectives and policies.

Today he launched a blame game tactic to take your eye off the ball again as to who shrunk the economy. It must have been his predecessor and the current flock of Republicans, it couldn't have been him. After all, he has only been in office for four years responsible for the slowest recovery in the United States since World War II.

It first began with Carney in the press briefing room and then House Dem Leader Nancy Pelosi alleging that GOP feet-dragging during talks over the fiscal crisis and willingness to accept automatic defense cuts contributed to the economic squeeze.

Carney, however, glossed over the fact that both Democrats and Republicans agreed to the 2011 debt-ceiling legislation that set in motion more than $500 billion in defense cuts.

Pelosi further charged that "today's disappointing GDP report is a direct result of the economic uncertainty created by House Republicans' strategy of obstruction and manufactured crises."

Republicans accused the White House of having selective amnesia.

It is clear that Obama has zero interest in debt. He has stated that we don't have a spending problem. But the facts are we are $16 trillion in debt, we are on the path to Europe and Obama is taking us there with his magic.

Who was it that shrunk the economy?

FAT-SHAMING

Manasota Key FL (Storch Report) January 26, 2013 -- Imagine going to your local supermarket and approaching someone you might think is obese and making a derogatory comment to shame them into slimming down.

Or, sitting alongside an obese man who is spilling over into your seat on a cross country flight and suggesting he might consider buying two seats on his next flight.

A bio-ethicist is now suggesting it is a social responsibility to participate in what he is calling 'Fat-Shaming' to encourage Americans to reduce their BMI.

I don't know how you socially participate in this not so politically correct process without spending some time at your dentist repairing the end result of your comments.

It sounds to me like part of a socialist agenda, perhaps it's hidden in the thousands of pages of Obamacare where it is the citizen's responsibility to shame their fellow Americans to do what's right for the nation because their obesity is costing us all mucho bucks.

The bio-ethicist draws the analogy to smoking, claiming this is what happened with the anti-smoking movement, we made it embarrassing to smoke. Of course we also banned it from most public places, even though more women are smoking today than yesterday.

Perhaps we should require all door jams be reduced in size so that only slim people can get through and the fat one's that try to get through have to be extracted with the jaws of life. I mean, after all how embarrassing would that be?

However, I do get confused at times with this political correctness of today's social thinking. It seems they tell me the country leans to the right of center and I seem to think it's going the other way.

Same sex marriage appears to be okay and growing exponentially from state to state. After all the president says it's okay and so does the Veep, but they only see that social issue from the perspective of votes.

When it comes to same sex marriage, isn't there a health component here similar to smoking cigarettes? Isn't there a greater risk of AIDS among those that participate in this form of behavior?

And when it comes to guns, banning or controlling to protect our children, how hypocritical can we be? Since Roe V Wade was passed the United States government killed 55 million human beings and the beat goes on. There was an 18% increase in abortions last year over the previous year.

Governments are banning the smoking of cigarettes in public places, salt in restaurants, big drink sodas and restricting pain medication in hospitals. Government has no faith in the minds of the electorate, except for their vote which they control through brain washing.

I'm appalled by the word social, because if I add three letters to the word it comes out socialist and reminds me of the president of the United States.

Political correctness is the term under which this movement has evolved, or in 'Fat-Shaming', political incorrectness which is now deemed correct, but it is really more of what we have seen in our past history. The subliminal involvement of government controlling people? Fascism, Communism and Nazism in Europe during the 30's comes to mind.

Individuals are bamboozled every day by con artists, but so are nations by governments that are allowed to grow too large and powerful. Perhaps we should use some 'Fat-Shaming' on them.

FOOT LONG SUBWAYS ARE AN INCH SHORT OF WHAT THEY SHOULD BE

Englewood FL (Storch Report) January 24, 2013 -- When I buy a sandwich at Subway, which I often do, I get a six inch sub and if the foot long sub is now an inch short of 12 inches, which is what's being alleged, what happens to the six inch sub, now already an inch short and the sandwich chef doesn't cut the loaf in the middle, am I paying for more inches than I'm getting?

I doubt whether the sandwich chef is measuring to make sure they are cutting my sandwich in the middle. If this were the case the chef would have to calculate that the 12 inch sub is an inch short, then would have to measure my six inch sandwich at 5 and a half inches in order to give me half of the foot-long sandwich which has been calculated as being an inch short.

I mean, after all, if I am on a fixed income, I could be losing as much as two inches on a sub by buying the six inches rather than the 12 inches, which I am told is already short by one inch, possibly because the loaf shrinks during the baking process, and the chef's human error of not cutting the loaf in the middle.

I'm really concerned about this, not because I want to sue Subway, I just want to be treated as fairly as the foot long patron who is already an inch short, as compared to me who is buying the 6 inch sub which is really a 5 and a half inch sub, but now I am

subject to the chef's possible human error and I could come up 2 inches short.

You see it really gets more complicated than that. When I get home I cut the alleged six inch sub in half and it makes two luncheons for me. Now if I cut the sub correctly, I thought I was getting a 3 inch sub. But I'm really not because the 6 inch sub is only 5 and a half inches and if I calculate my own human cutting error I may be getting a two inch sub one day and a 2 and a half inch sub the next day.

Now, I really got a lot of comfort the other day when I found out that the American Heart Association gave Subway the healthy heart symbol; however, I am now wondering whether it's because they were cutting down on the number of inches they were serving ergo the calories.

I don't know about you, but from now on I'm going to Subway with a tape measure, I'm determined not to be short inched, no matter how good these subs are for me.

I'M GETTING LONELY IN THIS BIG HOUSE

Washington DC (Storch Report) January 14, 2013 -- I'm beginning to feel sorry for President Obama. During his last news conference of his first term today he admitted to the nation, "I'm getting lonely in this big house."

His confession came during a question from the media as to whether he has been too insular during his first term.

He said, "I'm a friendly guy, I like a good party. We invite members of Congress here all the time, some choose not to come," he said.

He noted, however, that we have 'stark differences in policy.' He even said, "Some blast me for being a big spending socialist."

Of course he didn't admit to being one, nor did anyone in the media have the guts to ask him if it were true.

Nevertheless, he was apparently smarting a bit from the criticism.

Now the sad part to addressing the 'insular' question came when he said, "You know my girls are getting big and they don't want to hang out with me much anymore, maybe I'll call up someone from Congress to play cards with me."

It was then that he dropped the line, "I'm getting lonely in this big house."

Tears began to flow from the ranks of the hardcore female press corps.

It was the only soft moment in a rather contentious, testy news conference where he arrogantly reiterated throughout, "that he would not negotiate with Republicans over the federal debt ceiling."

He said that Social Security checks would be delayed and the nation could enter a new recession if Republicans do not agree to allow for more US borrowing.

Obama said Republicans "will not collect a ransom in exchange for not crashing the American economy," continuing to ratchet up the rhetoric over the looming deadline to raise the $16.4 trillion debt ceiling.

Anyone for cards with Barack, 'the big spending Socialist?'

STORCH REPORT: BIDEN AND OBAMA AT LUNCH WITH BO

Washington DC (Storch Report) January 1, 2013 -- I don't know if you are aware of it, or not, but Vice President Joe Biden and President Barack Hussein Obama have lunch almost on a weekly basis when they are both in town.

Realizing this I called up Jay Carney, White House Press Secretary and asked him if there was some way that I could get some idea of what they talk about at lunch.

I thought it would make a great feature. In other words, without being part of a lunch, could I talk to someone who might give me some insight into what was actually going on between Barack and Joe?

Carney gave me that smirk and sneer where the left side of his lip slips upward in disdain and I knew I had stepped out of bounds and it was then he suggested that I talk to the White House Chief Dog, Bo.

He thought this would put me off, but I countered and asked if Bo was frequently at lunch with the two? He assured me he was there whenever they had lunch. "Joe likes dogs," he said.

I'm sure Carney thought he was pulling a fast one on me, referring me to the family dog.

So, we set up a meeting with Bo. We got along swell and worked-out a communications plan Carney doesn't have with the White House Press Corps.

I would ask questions and the two of us set-up a glossary of terms and signals for Bo's body language and his answers that would disclose what was being discussed at lunch.

It basically consisted of barks, blinks, sneezes, tail wags, right and left paw motions, shakes and farts, all of which told me what was going on.

The most recent lunch took place after Obama's abbreviated vacation to Hawaii, returning to address a deal on the fiscal cliff.

Bo and I met in the Rose Garden, and I told him I needed some basic background information about the relationship, like what did Joe call Obama?

Does he call him Barack, Hussein, or, Obama?

Bo farted at each name. Apparently Joe doesn't like any of these names, in fact, Bo said, he often makes a Freudian slip and calls him Hillary.

Joe calls him Mr. President, after all this is what Joe was aspiring to call himself, Bo said.

It was rather amazing to me that Bo was so candid, as compared to the rest of the family and it was then that he disclosed that Obama was going to turn over negotiations to Joe for the fiscal cliff, and this happened at the last luncheon.

Bo said Obama doesn't like talking to members of Congress other than Speaker of the House John Boehner, who cries a lot. Obama likes weakness, Bo said.

Bo said Obama is not a people person, he likes Campaign-style town hall meetings. "You know he was a community organizer," Bo said.

I pointed out to Bo that this fiscal cliff crisis was going on for some four years and wondered whether or not he thought this was nothing but Kabuki Theater?

He then said he would have to check with his pan-Asian doggies. I said pan-Asian? He said yes, we don't call Chinese restaurants Chinese anymore, it is not politically correct. However, he did note that they still use cats in their chicken chow mien. He said he got this from good sources from the cat house he goes to on K Street.

I said Chinese? He said Chinese, Japanese, all the same – one from column A another from column B.

I asked Bo what he thought Joe would be able to accomplish on the fiscal cliff.

Bo said the Prez would cave on the $250,000 tax increase on the rich and take it to $450,000, but would insist in that package that he would be allowed to spend to put the nation $4 trillion more into further debt.

Bo said these guys are big government with entitlements.

"You wouldn't believe the entitlements I have," Bo said. "I have full run of the house, the Rose garden, Michelle's vegetable garden and I even piss on the tomatoes. I really hope the White House kitchen washes them off before they donate them to the kid's school."

I asked Bo one last question, why did Obama win reelection?

He answered in one word, "Adolescence."

"Guys like you are too mature to even understand what you created. You thought it was all about the Constitution and right and wrong, honor, duty, country and so on but you gave your kids everything they wanted and they became accustomed to it and that is precisely what they want and what Obama promises. That is how he got reelected," Bo said.

"Hey," he said, "I enjoyed our chat," he pawed me his card, "Here's how you can reach me, you don't have to go through that kid in the press office, we can meet at the cat house on K Street."

TWO PRECOCIOUS 10-YEAR-OLDS' DISCUSSING THE STATE OF THE UNION

Washington DC (Storch Report) Dec 30, 2012 -- "Homer, what do you think about what's going on these days, you know, about the fiscal cliff and all that other stuff?"

"Well, Gwendolyn, it does remind me a bit of our lower class peers, you know the middle class down there playing in the sand box, tinkling and throwing sand in each other's' face."

"I mean after all Homer, if they call us 'precocious' at our age what do they call the president and members of congress at their stage of life?"

"Obnoxious, ego-maniacal, with early onset of dementia looking forward to collecting the entitlements they voted in for themselves as early as they can get it."

"Oh, Homer you're so cynical and pessimistic. After all they we're considerate enough to provide Plan B for me and provide that Glock pistol to you so you can protect us from those crazies."

"That's true Gwen, but I think the NRA was instrumental in getting me the Glock, and that Sandra Fluke, if that's what her name was, well, she helped you to do it three times a day."

"You're not complaining are you, Homer?"

"Don't get me wrong, as a matter of fact my parents are out of the house this afternoon and we could have a matinee?"

"Homer, I remember when I was five and a matinee was an ice cream sundae at Hagen-Das."

"Yes, those were the good old days. I guess we are growing up too soon, but we have to take on responsibilities, under this Marxist regime, sooner than later, and plan on retirement later than sooner, and our middle class peers down there in the sandbox; poor souls, will be doing tomorrow, despite what the president promised, what they are doing today, pissing on each other."

"Homer, let's go to your parents' house."

"Did you take Plan B?"

"I don't have to take it until tomorrow morning."

SUPERFICIALITY

Manasota Key FL (Storch Report) November 27, 2012 -- I have thought about this word over my lifetime and have never written a word about it until now, because it's a scene I have seen all too often and a trait I of behavior I characteristically abhor.

When you think about the word, it smacks of phony-ism and one you wouldn't want to be associated with, but most of the people you associate with are superficial and perhaps, much to your own surprise, you might be one of them.

I mean, after all if you are one of those persons who really wants to be liked, accepted and invited to the 'in' parties of your peers, you are most likely superficial.

You really can't be liked if you speak your mind, thereby risking the possibility of being offensive.

And if you express your opinion and fail to use the platitudes of superficiality in a social environment, well, you are a suspect of individualism. And this personifies a person who expresses his or her opinion and doesn't pander to being nice for the sake of being liked.

I once worked for a former Assistant Secretary of State and we were in DC at a cocktail party one evening. We met at the bar, got a drink and he said to me, "Okay, let's work the room. I'll go this way, you go that way and we will meet back here in a half-an-hour and go to dinner." He smoked, but never carried cigarettes. He carried

a gold Dunhill lighter in his pocket to light up the ladies and then bummed a butt.

Superficiality is pervasive, it is not just a social thing, it is a business thing, it is a political thing, it's a global thing and it is a family thing, and when the only purpose in life is being nice to be liked, and not true unto one self, and you go home feeling nauseous, you are most likely superficial and recognize it.

However, conversely being superficial can make you feel good, because being liked is a high. Take for example Jill Kelley the Tampa Bay socialite tangentially associated in the Petraeus extramarital affair that reached into the social strata of DC; she even received the second highest civilian award from the military for being superficial, among other things.

Jill's Consul Role. An honorary one at that from South Korea, which was passed along by Petraeus, was revoked this week because she allegedly tried to milk it for $80 M in some deal to open doors that she couldn't.

If you are looking for the definition of superficiality, Kelley personifies a recent example of it, along with the generals she cultivated, a CIA Director, doctors, a bright military, author-mistress, all with trails leading to the White House.

When popularity fades into reality perhaps then too will superficiality, but then again don't look for that to happen too soon.

WHITE HOUSE HAS BECOME A REALITY TV SHOW WITH CHOTSKIES

Washington DC (Storch Report) November 8, 2012 -- The White House is looking more like a reality TV show with lots of chotskies.

I believe President Obama runs the Oval Office much the way ABC and Barbara Walters runs The View with lots of chotskies, that's how you improve your Neilson ratings.

Tickets are hard to get for the View, Ellen, Katie and those other TV shows that give away gifts to the audience and to some unfortunate guests that had a sad story to tell.

It makes you wonder is that where the Obama campaign got the idea of how to win this election. After all, he and Michelle appeared on two of these shows, the Katie debut, perhaps came too late for such an appearance, or I am sure he and Michelle would have been there. After all it was ABC.

The chotskies we are talking about are translated to entitlements when you get to the nation's capital.

But you see we all want to get something for nothing. But we know in reality there is no free lunch.

The TV shows we have mentioned are enticing because of the chotskies (entitlements such as social security, Medicare, food stamps, Obamacare) deliver little substance with respect to

content and the shows profit as a result of subliminal ad promo's and the audience appeal to get something for nothing.

A society created from the essence of the Obama administration formula of giveaways, is kind of a disguised concept of socialism. A campaign formula that you must give Obama credit for because that is his legacy of his first term, Campaigner in Chief.

They did the East Wing as a sitcom, they should do the Oval Office as a reality TV show. Perhaps a love affair between Barbara Walters and Obama could spice things up.

Obama dumbed-down his campaign to his base. He reached his voting base by appearing on the View, Ellen, Letterman, and Leno while Romney tried to reach the people face to face and appeal to their sophistication as a gentleman.

There is no room for a gentleman in today's politics.

And now we are trying to analyze what happened. Obama saw it as a TV show appealing to those that watch it on simple shows and Romney sought a higher level of thought, but the votes were not there.

And so now we have what we have. Is that much like it is what it is? Well whatever it is, it all seems pretty dumb to me and not productive for America.

Perhaps someone can make some money out of a White House Reality TV Show, produce some jobs and improve the economy in a dumb way.

OBAMA SHOULD LAUGH-A-LOT TUESDAY

Washington DC (Storch Report) October 14, 2012 -- President Obama should take a page from VP Joe Biden's debate book next Tuesday and laugh his way through the town hall style meeting rather than not showing up.

He should look to the heavens for direction, to the floor for distraction, throw his hands up in the air, flail his arms in his opponents face and giggle a lot while he's talking.

It may seem bizarre, but it worked for Joe. It might work for Obama too, after all Joe did better than he in the first debate and it sure distracts from a failed record of the last four years.

It seems to me, even without these tactics, Obama is not running to be reelected, he's running to see that Romney is defeated.

There is a difference. For if this were not true, why would he and his Chicago-style campaign loony toon operatives be delivering character assignation charges against Romney such as Bain Capital outsourcing allegations, tax return charges, offshore investment allegations, accusations of being a felon, killing an employee dying of cancer and avoid the issues at hand such as Benghazi-gate?

My gosh, when Benghazi-gate surfaces Tuesday Obama should jump up and down and stomp his feet like a two-year-old,

flailing his arms declaring, "Unfair, unfair" to moderator Candy Crowley of CNN. This would be much better than a Biden giggle or smirk.

Biden disclosed last Thursday during the Biden, Ryan debate, "We (meaning he and Obama) were not told they (meaning the Benghazi Consulate and the State Department) wanted more security,"

This statement was tantamount to the White House throwing Secretary of State Hillary Clinton under the bus. The quick response from the administration and the White House appeared to be transparent, but with politicized messages that continued to be in conflict with the State Department, and intelligence departments. The conflicting statements have continued now for more than a month, suggesting cover-up.

Four Americans died, including a US Ambassador in Benghazi and Biden laughed about it during a debate with Ryan.

The crisis can only be described as a cluster fu__. Oh, that's okay to say, after all Biden said to Obama when Obamacare was to be signed, "This is a big Fu_____ deal."

Biden in case you hadn't noticed is gaffe prone. He was in Danville when he said, "We can win North Carolina again" he told a crowd, forgetting that he was in Virginia. I wouldn't suggest Obama take this route on Tuesday.

Obama, however, does need Biden's body language distraction, even though it might make him look like he has Tourette's Syndrome, after all there are 23 million people out of work and the deficit is at $1.1 Trillion and all of this came about on his watch.

REST IN PEACE

Manasota Key FL (Storch Report) September 24, 2012 -- There seems to be a lot of people dying these days, and a lot of people saying after they pass, Rest in Peace.

I always had a problem with this phrase because by definition 'resting' is a state characterized by minimal function and metabolic activities . . . you know, like sleep and then you wake up?

You could also look at it as a place for resting or lodging, like Motel 6.

In both instances you wake up and are still alive after 'resting.'

The one that really gets me is 'Rest in Peace' and that is defined as the repose of death.

I mean, in this state the person is not resting, the person is dead.

Resting implies one is going to wake up. My father used to fall asleep watching TV, my mother used to say go to bed George. He would wake up and say, "I'm just resting my eyes," then he would go to bed.

Perhaps it should be lie in Peace, Peace in the Depth of the Sea or Rest in Your Cremains.

Words in the English language are at best mystifying.

Oh, with the multiple meanings of the English language and the grammar, which I don't pay much attention to, as long as I am sending and you are receiving; I feel sorry for those immigrants who cannot a speak a' the English and want to take on the challenge.

Here is a non sequitur for you in this piece; let's see if we can make it work in some way to segue to resting.

Recently the word antecedent popped up in the media, having to do something with President Obama, and I am sure he knows little about antecedent's unless it has something to do with show business.

In grammar, an antecedent is a noun, noun phrase, or clause to which an anaphor refers in coreference.

For example, in the passage "I did not see John because he wasn't there," "John" is the antecedent of the anaphor "he"; together "John" and "he" are called a coreference because they both refer to the same thing (in this case, a particular person).

The word "antecedent" begins with the prefix "ante-", meaning "before", because almost always the antecedent occurs before the anaphor.

"John" and "He" should Rest in Peace.

THE OUTSIDE INSIDE GUY WE SHOULD PLEASE – PUT HIM OUTSIDE

Washington DC (Storch Report) September 20, 2012 -- He said from the outside when he got inside that he would change it, but when he got inside he said it could only be changed from the outside.

Five days before he took the office he holds, he told America he was going to transform it, and we trusted this to mean it had something to do with hope and change.

We thought he was one of us, but then he started apologizing for us, like we did something wrong.

When he was outside he told Joe the Plumber that if you made it, I want to take some of your money and redistribute it to give someone else a shot. Joe didn't like that.

It was a promise he made and continues to pitch, redistribution of wealth that he has yet to achieve.

When he was outside he said he was going to be transparent, when he got inside he became so opaque there was a run on cataract operations.

When outside we thought that when inside he would govern on the basis of his promises, but we didn't realize until he was inside that he couldn't get out of his campaign mode.

It became clear that promises made outside, not fulfilled inside, and develops a Pinocchio nose and what it represents.

Duplicitous remarks outside segues to duplicitous remarks inside.

We thought when he was outside that he was going to represent all the people, like the oath of office says, but when he got inside he created class warfare and focused on the middle class.

But even they, although pleased to be the focus of his attention were but pawns and found they would be paying a tax, which he promised they wouldn't, for a socialistic healthcare program.

When you are outside in order to get inside you say things you can no longer say when you are inside.

And, when you are inside you say things you wouldn't say outside, but you like it so much inside, that you will say anything to stay there, rather than be outside.

I don't know about you, but I'm getting confused; however, I know who should be outside.

THE SOLUTION IS WHITE HOUSE BEER

Washington DC (Storch Report) Sep 2, 2012 -- Obama has the solution for himself to what's Ale – ing the country – White House Beer.

Now, if he only had the creativity and business acumen to recognize it, he's got the solution to jobs and the economy right under his nose.

He should develop a business from his personal pleasure: The 1600 Pennsylvania Avenue Brewery. It would provide jobs, stimulate the economy and generate profits so he can redistribute wealth to the middle class. It might even create enough of a buzz among the people for a recovery to get reelected.

However, in order to do this he must recognize the word serendipity. Originally Obama developed his concept of home brewing to resolve his own personal problems and did so with little transparency. But White House Beer could be the alcoholic solution to the nation's problems.

But he, the community organizer, needs a businessman to work with him, perhaps he should call on Mitt Romney?

Obama had three different brewskis developed by his kitchen cabinet and found that if you had enough beers by the end of the day you no longer gave a damn about jobs or economic recovery.

One beer is Honey Brown Ale the other Honey Porter and the president can now top the evening off with a Honey Blonde, a recent line extension, and then mutter that old Jackie Gleason line, "How sweet it is!"

You see the honey comes from a bee hive in Michelle's special South Lawn White House garden, which was developed to promote healthy drinking.

Actually, Michelle developed the garden to promote healthy eating but Obama corrupted the process by buying a home brewing kit for the kitchen, and put the staff to work fermenting Ale, then everyone was able to put a buzz on to take their minds off the economy.

Using alcohol to resolve problems is not new for presidents. George Washington brewed beer and distilled whiskey at Mt. Vernon across the Potomac River in Virginia and Thomas Jefferson made wine down at his Monticello estate, but this is the first time beer has been brewed in the White House.

Ale to the Chief!

I WANT TO GO ON VACATION WITH PRINCE HARRY!

London (Storch Report) August 24, 2012 -- Imagine what it must be like to go on vacation with Prince Harry; I couldn't compete with a 27-year-old Royal military stud, but I sure could live vicariously as a voyeur to his escapades.

On Harry's recent Las Vegas vacation last week there was the pool party with Olympic champ Lochte – I hope he didn't pee in the pool, because that's what he admits to doing — until 3 AM in the morning with a bevy of bikini-clad voluptuous beauties, which was followed or preceded by a Billiard table strip tourney where it appeared everyone lost, because they all were naked, including most notoriously, the Prince.

Harry is a fun guy, who everyone seems to love no matter what he does; he is the true Teflon Prince and hardly a chip off the old cad of a father, who bores the world.

Queen Elizabeth must be betwixt and between a son and a grandson as to which to endorse for Royal behavioral approval.

I mean after all, does the Queen really want to endorse a cad-of-a son in Charles, who she doesn't even want to be King, or endorse a Playboy Prince of a grandson that seems to give the world a smile on their faces although it might be hard to break a wrinkle on Grandmas.

There's saving grace my lord, Prince William, the princely one married to Kate, comes before Harry in the ascendency to the throne.

Nevertheless the story is out that Harry has been recalled from his raucous Vegas holiday to face censure, by both Queen Grandma and the military, the former to be more of a punishment than the latter.

The Daily, which I subscribe to, gave us their creative insight into the Captains Mass Harry is likely to face when he appears before the Queen at Buckingham Palace to get his dressing down:

"Little Prince Harry has landed you in big trouble, young man.

"For once, I can say I'd prefer it if you were wearing a Nazi uniform.

"I understand pool, and this is NOT what's meant by ball-in-hand

"Just who do you think you are? Pippa?

"You skew-whiff codswollop has really whined this duffer."

That's all I've got to say about that; until I've got something more to say about Prince Harry's next chapter.

I mean, after all he's fun and brings a smile to everyone's face but Grandmas!

TIME TO BRING BACK COASTAL WATCHERS?

Manasota Key FL (Storch Report) Aug 15, 2012 -- There was a story published this week in The Washington Free Beacon written by Bill Gertz (8/14/12) with a headline "Silent Running" and it was about a Russian nuclear powered attack submarine armed with long-range cruise missiles and it operated in the Gulf of Mexico for several weeks undetected in strategic US waters and wasn't confirmed until after it left the region.

The story received virtually little attention by the main stream media, perhaps, due to the political hoopla surrounding Romney's nomination of Paul Ryan as his pick for the GOP VP nominee – all of this much to the fortuitous good luck of the Obama Administration.

We didn't miss the story as our website still so testifies.

The significance of this breach of security is no small matter. For the incursion, according to Gertz, in the Gulf took place at the same time Russian strategic bombers made incursions into restricted US airspace near Alaska and California in June and July, highlighting growing military assertiveness by Moscow since Vladimir Putin, an ex-KGB intelligence officer, has returned to power as President.

Shades of the Cold War returning?

The patrol by the Russians exposed what US officials said were deficiencies in US anti-submarine warfare capabilities.

You see the military is facing cuts under the Obama administration of defense spending by $487 billion over the next 10 years.

The article reported that the Navy is in charge of detecting submarines, especially those that sail near US nuclear missile submarines, and undersea sensors and satellites to locate and track them.

They said the fact that the Akula, which is a class of Russian Stealth Sub, was not detected in the Gulf is a cause for concern, US officials were reported as saying.

Now if you think it was a concern for them, think about me. I'm sitting on a barrier reef on the shores of the Gulf of Mexico.

Up until this revelation, my only concerns were Manta Rays, Sting Rays and Sharks – now I have to look out for Russian nuclear attack subs?

I thought I was being protected by my government. But on 9/11 I found out that wasn't true.

On the day of the unbelievable, I said to my wife," Aren't we lucky to be living here." Before we lived 30 miles outside of New York.

The next day I found my sleepy barrier reef on the West Coast of Florida, was just a 15 minute car ride from where Mohamed Ata and Marwan al-Shehhi, the terrorists piloting the two jets that brought down the World Trade Center killing nearly 3,000, trained at a local airport in Venice to execute the worst attack against the US.

And now, I discover Russian nuclear attack subs are patrolling off my beaches, and my government doesn't know anything about it until after they left my home port, confirming the incursion. I mean, after all, do I have any claims of trespassing under international law?

The story that goes with the beach house that I bought and expanded up and back, was that it was a coastal watch for German subs in World War II. And they tell me a few were spotted.

I immediately thought of destiny. Could I be destined for greatness in my twilight years?

I thought about writing President Obama and suggesting he restore, the Coastal Watchers, circa 1939, prior to the US entry into World War II. They made a significant contribution during the war, and in this time of budget cuts I thought I could make a contribution, especially with my strategic location. And, I would donate my time and service.

After all I would be a perfect volunteer, I served in the United States Navy during the Cold War and did so on the USS Howard W. Gilmore AS 16 a sub tender out of Key West Florida.

So I know something about subs, I saw them dock alongside my ship.

I don't know if you know anything about the Coastal Watchers of WW II, but they were heroes, they were posted in remote areas to watch for enemy activity and report by radio. The most famous coast watchers were those of the Australian "Ferdinand" organization, which dated back to 1939 and consisted of reservists recruited from among planters, colonial officials and missionaries in areas like the Solomon's, New Guinea and the Bismarck's. They provided air forces at Guadalcanal several hours' warning of incoming raids.

These Coastal Watchers were portrayed in some popular films of the times, like PT 109, Father Goose, South Pacific, and the Wackiest Ship in the Army, among others.

Well I thought with the budget crisis that we are facing I could do something similar here in the Gulf of Mexico.

After all, our security has been breached and no one seems to be paying attention but me. I don't want to be compensated, a few residuals from movie rights would be okay.

I would need something more than the radio, binoculars and computer that I have. Perhaps some sensor devices for stealth detection that don't work and an old 45 side arm that I did carry in the Navy, which I understand has been determined to be the best today, would be okay.

Just a thought Mr. President, they say what goes around comes around.

BADMINTON WAS NOT NAMED GOOD MINTON FOR A REASON

In My Backyard On Manasota Key Fl (Storch Report) August 1, 2012-- Well, one of my favorite Olympic sports badminton, as you know if you've been reading this column, soared into the news within the past 24 hours because some players representing the Chinese, South Korea and Indonesia, were tanking the game so they could get into a favorable flight, giving them a better chance of winning the gold.

The IOC Badminton World Federation four member disciplinary committee saw this, after deliberating for five hours, as a flagrant violation of Olympic rules and banned eight players from the Olympics.

It was a blow to the badminton backyard barbecue community of families across the world.

Imagine, badminton cheating in the Olympics, who would have thunk?

Only the night before there was that China girl who beat all male world records in swimming and won a gold medal, then a second the next day, and now a controversy is surrounding her about doping.

Oh, not because she is dumb, there are no dumb Chinese, but because she was possibly cheating.

Cheating is rampant today. They tell me we humans cheat to win. They say it starts in school and one cheats throughout their academic career. They say we cheat in business, sports, politics and all other aspects of life – even badminton.

I guess we don't have to worry about doping in badminton, for it doesn't take much energy to hit a shuttlecock over the net, especially if you are tanking the game with the intent of hitting it under the net.

I understand that thing that they are hitting the racquet with is called the shuttlecock. I think they shortened the name to shuttle, to clean up the game.

I like going to barbecues and watching people play badminton, but now I better understand why they don't call it good Minton. It's because people cheat at the game. Wait until the IOC here's about these backyard violations!

Very frankly, I can think of better things to cheat at where the rewards are greater.

Oh well, back to the Olympics.

RAINING ON THE BORING BRITISH OLYMPIC PARADE

London (Storch Report) July 29, 2012 -- I really don't mean to rain on anyone's parade, least of all the young world class athletes competing in the summer Olympic games, but I found the opening ceremonies to be a rather British bore and it appeared by their facial expressions, the Royal family agreed with me.

Perhaps the Queen was just a bit tired after jumping out of that Helicopter in that peach colored sparkle plenty dress and topper with James Bond?

The highlight of the Olympics so far was Lochte beating Phelps in the first swimming match and then being barred from wearing a red, white and blue mouth grill on the medal stand to accept the gold, all of this nonsensical officialdom while the Queen pulls off a phony parachute jumping stunt as a Bond girl.

After falling asleep somewhere between Harry Potter and Paul McCartney singing 'Hey Jude' in the opening ceremonies, I anxiously awaited the next few weeks of my most-favorite events: table tennis, badminton, skeet shooting, water polo, handball, canoe and kayak racing, judo, archery and the closing ceremony so I can go back to sleep.

Oh, but for the bloody boring British, the noon day sun the guards stand in at Buckingham Place until they faint, and the constant rain, what will I do for entertainment until the next Royal wedding?

GARBAGE

Manasota Key Fl (Storch Report) July 13, 2012 -- I don't know about you, but I don't care much about garbage, other than it's me that takes it out to be picked up; where it goes after that I leave to somebody else to deal with.

My wife tells me garbage should be separated so that it can be recycled, you know for all those environmental reasons, which very frankly I don't give much credence to.

And she says it's important to put the paper and cardboard in one bag and to not put envelopes with cellophane windows in the same bag, they go into the garbage. Then the bottles, cans and plastic goes in another bag. All of this is then transferred to multi-colored bins, in the garage, before it is taken out to the street for pick-up by Waste Management.

The garbage goes in a big green bin, but I sometimes sneak things into this bin that doesn't belong – I learned this from the garbage men. The bottles, plastic and cans go into the red bin and the cardboard and paper without those envelopes, with cellophane windows, go into the green bin.

Now that I have done the sorting of a mailman with garbage, which the mailman does less of with mail these days, I take it out to the street.

And it is there that I find the garbage man takes the red bin dumps it into the green bin, mixing it with my recyclables,

dumps it into the WM green truck, and compacts it into one bail of mush.

I am devastated, all of my recyclable sorting is now in one bail of mush.

Now I knew another truck was coming along for garbage to pick up that big green bin. I couldn't help but wonder where that bin was going – was it going to that same pile of my recyclable pile of mush?

Now, I really never cared a tinker's damn about this crap, but I have put some effort into this recyclable trash and it seems to me these guys in those green uniforms are breaking the rules.

However, while watching this green process transform before my eyes I somehow had visions of President Carter, lobbying for the Nobel Peace Prize, much the way Phil Rizzuto lobbied for the Hall of Fame, and both got what they sought, and then there was former VP Al Gore receiving a Nobel Prize for environmental warming, in the midst of a controversy about whether there was such a thing or not, and then President Obama getting the Nobel Peace Prize, shortly after entering office, while engaged in at least two wars.

I sometimes wonder what I'm doing taking out carefully recyclable trash, after all isn't all of this just garbage in and garbage out in just one big mush.

You know, I could be writing another column for you with the time I waste on garbage on a weekly basis?

A TAX IS WHAT IT IS, BUT THEN AGAIN WHAT IS IT, IF IT'S A PENALTY?

Washington DC (Storch Report) July 5, 2012 -- I can understand a President not understanding what is, is. But not understanding what a tax is, is troublesome.

I thought I would try to be helpful to these two Harvard law school graduates by putting it in the simplest of terms: tax is what pays one of your salaries now, and could pay the other tomorrow.

It is what you collect from the people you serve, fly around the world on Air Force One apologizing for us, and taking vacations on us with all the perks that go along with the job.

It is what you collect from the people to run up a nearly $16 trillion deficit, spending more than you take in, providing entitlements like Obamacare, and therein lies the focus of your confusion despite all your learning; you just don't know what to call what you passed, when you promised that it was not what it is — a tax. It seems the people who pay what you propose know better than you what it is.

That word is, is difficult to understand. It was a significant contribution from a previous president.

A tax is what a liberal president spends on an entitlement bill, called ironically, an affordable health care act, costing in the trillions, instead of focusing on a recession and jobs, but then spends

more tax payer money through a stimulus program that fails and sustains an unemployment rate of more than 8.2 % for a first term in office.

A tax is what a liberal president wants more of by lobbying for redistribution of wealth, taxing those that pay the most more, but then discovers from the Supreme Court that when he promised no taxes to the middle class because he had their backs, they tripped him up by declaring that Obamacare could only be constitutional as a tax and would be unconstitutional as a mandate under the Commerce Clause.

It brought back memories of a former president who had trouble with a two letter word, is.

The curve ball from the Supreme Court was thrown by conservative Chief Justice John Roberts who promised Congress during his confirmation hearings that he would only call balls and strikes, but he is now like a tenured teacher – no one can get rid of him.

You see it was he that said Obamacare, along with the Courts liberal justices, declared that it was unconstitutional as a mandate under the commerce clause, but then they re-wrote it as a tax to make it constitutional thus confusing, attorneys, a constitutional lawyer/president and a candidate.

I am sure you now know that I'm talking about the confused presidential candidates, President Barack Obama and presumed GOP candidate Gov. Mitt Romney, who had his own version of Obamacare known as Romney care when he was governor of Massachusetts.

When the Supreme Court ruling came out the White House insisted that it was not a tax it was a "penalty."

After all, it never would have passed the then democratically controlled Congress had it been presented as a tax. But then again no one read the 2700 page bill at the time it was passed to know what it was. A Romney etch-a-sketch spokesman called it a "penalty" seemingly agreeing with the Obama campaign, but then Romney himself corrected that calling it a "tax." He said the Supreme Court

called it a tax and it's a tax. Tonight Romney announced he was revamping his communications team.

Today the Obama campaign said again it was a "penalty" and argued that the Solicitor General who argued the case before the Supreme Court for the administration said it was a penalty. This is incorrect, transcripts show that the SG argued in behalf of Obama that it was a tax, making Obama a hypocrite.

It has all the makings of an Abbott & Costello skit of "Who's On First."

I'll bet even Monica Lewinsky knew she had to pay a tax to have her dress cleaned.

BIG NANNY

Washington DC (Storch Report) June 14, 2012 -- What we the people need are more Nanny's in public office to protect us from ourselves.

I know I don't eat enough broccoli, in fact I don't eat any, and I know how good it is for me.

I have a feeling that what I need is some form of legislation to force me to eat more broccoli.

It's a classic example of what we need in this country more smart leaders who know better than we what's good for us like, Nanny Michele and her garden, and Barack Obama and Nanny Bloomberg of New York.

These are the people that really have the pulse and the health of our nation at their fingertips.

I have discovered that they can tell how healthy we are by the way we look, and if we are fat, as most of the nation is, that's not healthy and it doesn't look good. Just by looking at you they can probably figure out your BMI.

Perhaps Adolph Hitler wasn't that far off the mark when he promoted the concept of a Blond Aryan race, after all they sure did look healthy.

Let's face it these political leaders of our times only have our best interests in their hearts.

President Obama is forcing all Americans, with good intent, to purchase health insurance, perhaps there's something in that

legislation where I'll be forced to eat broccoli that's good for me, I certainly hope so.

And if I travel to New York more often I'll be able to cut back on my sodium, be able to check the amount of calories in the food I order before I make a selection, obtain smaller portions of soda – no more giant gulps in those 4 star restaurants Bloomberg frequents – smaller portions of milk, and have the pop taken out of my corn. And, thanks to Nanny Bloomberg, our lungs will be better, because no one can smoke anywhere.

I can envision Mayor Bloomberg standing behind Governor Chris Christie of neighboring New Jersey saying," I'll bet you can't see me, and if you can't, that's good!"

We really should embrace these legislative moves that are so good for us even though we may not like being told what to do. I mean, after all in retrospect wasn't your mother right most of the time, and even though you didn't listen to what she said?

I mean, we should really look at how well our politicians have handled their responsibilities, you know like jobs, the economy, housing and most of all our national debt to understand why they want to curb our excessive consumption. You don't see any extraordinary stimulus practices in their behavior and oh, look at how svelte they all are.

Now they tell us these enforced food moves are not only good for us, but they will result in lower health care costs. Oh, how wise they are.

I look forward to the day when the government makes more decisions for me, relieving me from the stresses in my life to constantly make difficult decisions. For example, it would be a pleasure for me to be forced to buy a GM car made in China, because I still own a portion of the company, I think – but I don't seem to be getting any dividends.

I just hope there is a provision in Obamacare that allows for some form of behavior modification therapy for me to once again restore happiness in my life, while realizing all of this is so good for me.

THE OBAMA'S ARE BIG ON BROCCOLI BUT THEY DON'T LIKE BEETS

New York (Storch Report) May 29, 2012 -- I never thought it possible that an Obama could find a way to bash a Bush from a vegetable garden, but Michelle found a way today on The View.

Michelle told the giggling ga ga girls of The View, Whoopi, Barbara, Joy and Sherri, but for one, Elizabeth, who have a love-fest for the first family and provide an open-ended promotional platform for President Obama's reelection, that they love broccoli, but hate beets.

It was President George H. W. Bush that didn't like broccoli, he didn't say much about beets; nor did 'W' say anything about broccoli. But never let a good bash to a Bush go to waste, after all they are all part of the same family.

The first lady was there to ostensibly promote her veggie book, 'American Garden', but it was more likely to promote her 'American' husband and to distract from those Birthers' claims that he wasn't born in the United States and the failed presidential record he put together in the past three-and-a-half years.

From the broccoli of the White House garden came the distraction, deflection and deception not so subtly delivered.

When asked how she deals with the negative comments about her husband, she said, "I get to travel around the country a lot," – the taxpayers have noticed – and she implied that the people like her husband. "He keeps his eye focused on getting the country back on track." As though it somehow got off the rails before she and her husband arrived in the veggie garden.

Barbara wa wa, always seeking for a news break, while exposing her bias these days, said there were rumors that if her husband lost the election this year that she would enter politics.

Michelle, dismissed this suggestion out of hand, "I'm not interested in politics."

She did say during the interview process that politics was tough and that you needed a thick skin.

There was a lot of sucking up to the first lady by the Dems of The View, while the token Republican, Elizabeth, played her dutiful respectful role.

Back in the garden, Michelle was asked if she did any digging. "Oh, no I don't do any digging."

I guess that's only for Barbara.

The garden is a work of art, impeccably developed and cared for with walkways to search for the abundance of broccoli, with little room for beets, a show place for Michelle to tell the kids, the nation and the world how to eat, especially their veggies, while she and her husband sneak off and have hot dogs and hamburgers.

I guess it's all about the duplicity of having a veggie garden for show while secretly desiring that tasty food that is oh so bad for us according to the government.

I happen to like beets, but I can understand why the Obama's don't; they are red and red will cover the states on election eve.

EVOLUTION OF TIME PART II, GENDER NEUTRAL BATHROOMS

Manasota Key FL (Storch Report) May 17, 2012 -- This is an addendum to yesterday's column, that's how fast things are moving on gender issues; I discuss it yesterday and there's a new story on the issue today.

President Obama endorses same sex marriage and now there's a movement (pardon the pun) for gender neutral bathrooms in colleges.

It's not bad enough our colleges are so liberal that a recent survey disclosed that out of the top 35 colleges across this country only one conservative was selected as a commencement speaker this year, the rest were liberals; and now colleges are caving to student demands for neutral gender bathrooms.

I'll bet you think there's a non sequitur in the previous sentence? If so, think again!

Yes, the symbol above this column says what you think it means.

At the University of Maryland this month a student went on a hunger strike protesting for gender neutral bathrooms and the administration caved to his wishes. I don't know if it was a compassionate move to save the student from death from starvation, or to salvage his tuition.

Imagine the scenes tomorrow: A female walks into a gender neutral bathroom, picks a stall, sits down and hears this tapping.

She remembers the story about the tapping Congressman in a male airline terminal bathroom and says, "I'm of the female gender". And a voice comes back, "I'm tapping for the next stall".

How the police would pull a sting operation off in this bathroom, which will probably be unconstitutional in a gender neutral cultural, would be a case for the late Colombo to solve.

What is the motive for this scene? Is it to be more like Europe, where they do have those gender neutral Loos? Or, perhaps to save on the number of necessary bathrooms; but the size would need to be increased based on volume, especially for women?

Cultural confusion through the now acceptable evolution of the thought process has soared to the heights of the White House to the depths of our bathrooms.

If all of this is what one political party is now calling 'Forward", I'll take 'Backward' and separate me from her, him from me, her from her, and anything else that represents same sex gender in the bathroom.

VANILLA ICE CREAM AND CHOCOLATE SYRUP IS MY CHOICE

Manasota Key FL (Storch Report) April 26, 2012 -- Comparing presidential candidates to being vanilla, rocky road, tutti frutti ice cream or being cool, hip, flip and singing ballads is about as intelligent a way to vote for a candidate as the American public once did when it put a cool, hip, flip, glib black man without credible capabilities, qualifications or accomplishments in the White House.

The pundits today are comparing Mitt Romney to vanilla, President Obama to rocky road and Vice President Joe Biden to tutti frutti.

We don't know yet who Romney's running mate will be, but you can be sure the person will be labeled.

Whomever it might be, I hope the label used is chocolate syrup because vanilla ice cream and chocolate syrup is my dessert of choice.

Today the tutti frutti Veep, Joe Biden compared Obama to President Teddy Roosevelt's foreign policy and his quote about, "speaking softly and carrying a big stick."

"I promise you the president has a big stick." And then, with emphasis tutti frutti said, "I promise you."

Now when you are already a cool president, you don't need your Veep's faux pas, you get enough mentions on the late night talk shows and those comedian hosts:

"What's the difference between Obama and his dog Bo? Bo has papers." Jimmy Kimmel.

"Have you heard about McDonald's new Obama value meal? Order anything you want and the guy behind you will pay for it." Conan O'Brien.

It all follows that cool show business principal, "I don't care what you say, just mention my name.'

Labels dealing with the likes of jobs, economy, devalued homes and 401 K's, big government, foreign policy, wars, liberal's socialists, Marxists do not seem important.

Cool is the operative word.

Once there was a men's hair style that was 'cool' called a Duck's Ass (DA).

I'll have vanilla ice cream with chocolate syrup.

OBAMA'S SECRET SERVICE STIMULUS IN CARTAGENA; GSA PARTY BASH IN VEGAS

Cartagena Co (Storch Report) Ap 17, 2012 -- How does the average American wrap their minds around a Secret Service stimulus in Cartagena or nearly a million dollar party bash for a few in Vegas by employees of GSA while back home, people are without jobs, lost their homes, other homes are under water and their retirement plans are devalued?

I thought the stimulus money was spent?

I'm confused, but under these circumstances, do you want the government handling your health care?

Now there is media empathy for Secretary of State Hillary Clinton for her tiring global jaunts in behalf of the US, but perception is reality and she was photographed dancing and drinking at the Club Havana in Cartagena Sunday, after the Secret Service prostitution probe and the GSA party bash investigation was revealed.

What the hell she deserves this and more, albeit media reports only had her in the club for 30 minutes. Nevertheless it just added fuel to the perception this is a partying administration in dire times.

Things are not going well for Obama these days and perhaps they shouldn't base upon his performance, after all his office is where the buck stops . . . or, does it.

Someone that once occupied his office once said that; but those were different times and he was a different guy.

Perhaps there is too much stimulus going on these days fostered by the concept of liberal entitlements?

The GSA was so confident about what they were doing in Vegas, they posted photos and videos on social networks of the partying for about 300 GSA employees.

One of them, Jeffrey Neely, Western Regional Commissioner of GSA, who organized the more than $820,000 bash, was photographed by his wife sitting in a hot tub with two glasses of wine along side of him, but yesterday under the advice of counsel he took the 5th six times during a Congressional hearing investigating the boondoggle.

On Sunday Obama said he was going to be 'angry' if the alleged prostitution charges in Cartagena are 'true' involving his secret service agents.

'Angry' seems to be a mild liberal adjective to use under these circumstances.

I think I would be furious, I would look upon it as a serious security breach, a personal embarrassment to me and my country; but at the White House it is standard operating procedure to stall for time, use mild non-inflammatory words unless it's a racial issue, after all there is an investigation going on and it would be 'inappropriate' to comment before it is completed.

And, given enough time there must be someone else to blame for all of this. Bush must be around somewhere.

I NEVER GOT A LOTTERY TICKET

Manasota Key FL (Storch Report March 30, 2012 -- There has been a lot of hype about the mega million dollar lottery, the winner of which will be drawn this evening at 11 PM (DST), and the prize has now grown to $640 million.

That's a lot of money.

I don't gamble, now it's not that I haven't tried, but I found out early in life that I'm not a winner when it comes to the luck of the draw.

I have trouble winning playing the card game Kings on the Corner.

I once went to a business related Christmas function where everyone got a gift when their name was called.

When mine was called I received a dozen roll-on under arm deodorant bottles.

I had some relative guests visiting at the time from Europe and gave them some of my winnings.

A few months later I found out the product, which was in a test market at the time, had been withdrawn from the market and later discovered the product stained the clothes of my relatives.

So, with this kind of luck, I have decided not to by lotto tickets nor gamble.

But with all the hype around this mega million lotto, I had some thoughts about buying a ticket or two.

I quickly questioned my judgment and examined the facts.

First of all I don't have any luck when it comes to gambling and the odds of winning on this one for lucky persons are not very positive, what could it be for me with my track record? One who wins under arm deodorant and passes it along to relatives and it rots their clothes?

Then I thought about winning. What would I do with the money?

I would probably have to hire a financial adviser to help me manage the money. I would know more then he, and then have to manage him which would be an aggravation; I would want to take care of my family and that would cause more angst.

I would consider gifts to charity, but having chaired a contributions committee for a major corporation, I would consider most charities to be corrupt.

My wife would probably want a new house and I like it where I'm at.

Oh, there are other things I might consider, but then again I have all the gadgets and toys I need.

So, I came to the conclusion who needs it?

Nevertheless, when I went out to get the mail today in my street legal golf cart, I decided to take a ride to Circle K where they sell lotto tickets. I went there ostensibly to pick up some soda and a sandwich.

I did think of picking up a lotto ticket or two.

I think there was some malice of forethought in the back of my mind. Because there were some numbers in my pocket that I got off The Daily a news magazine I subscribe to and it gave me the numbers I intended to play, after all with my luck I couldn't trust myself to come up with the numbers.

When I approached Circle K I expected there to be lines outside waiting to by mega million lottery tickets.

There was no one. I picked up a 12 pack of orange soda, a sandwich and walked up to the check-out counter where there was

a sign, 'Florida does not participate in the mega million dollar lottery'.

I walked out of the store thinking to myself, 'what a lucky guy.'

Oh, the numbers I picked, in case you want to play them, were: 25 45 30 29 18 24 and 8 7 43 39 22 27. Good luck!

CHRISTIE'S GIRTH, GUTS AND GRAVITAS, THE CHOICE

Manasota Key FL (Storch Report) March 1, 2012 -- It seems to me that the process that the nation is going through to select a GOP presidential candidate through our primaries is now not only becoming laborious and boring but it is becoming destructive to the candidates and beneficial to the president most of the nation would like to rid themselves of.

Republican candidates for president have been vetted to the degree President Obama was not by the Democrats.

In the process they are cutting themselves apart fighting each other for the right to beat Obama while he is out collecting a billion dollars from his wealthy left wing supporters and the unions he paid back the last time during the auto industry bailout.

We know more about what we don't know about Obama than we know, and we found out all of what we don't know after he became president. Thank you Casey and Yogi.

And after the fact we found out this wasn't a good thing from the person we know little about because it was he that reported the state of the nation wasn't in a good place, but it wasn't his fault.

And so one might think what we are going through now with the Republicans might be positive due diligence for the process of selecting a president.

However, there are those political pundits that have analyzed all of this based on polls, statistics and have come to the conclusion the Republican process is bad for the "brand", something I didn't think of a president being, like a can of Budweiser.

I mean after all you can't beat-up on the brand without analysis and dissecting it like you would a product.

And so this is what the political pundits do with white boards, electronic computer screens showing stats from polls, focus groups, demographics, trends from the West, Middle America, the South and the East, White, Black, Hispanic, Immigrants and of course illegals.

The analysis is so intense and sophisticated that I've come to the conclusion it's meaningless.

So I did my own research down here in Southwest Florida talking to the real people who vote with their head not their emotion or intuition.

I also did what any sound pollster would do and went to redneck bars, a couple of hair salons, Wal-Mart and did some person on the street interviews on Dearborn.

What I found out was a striking difference from what those TV pundits learned with all of their sophisticated data, demographics, stats and analysis.

At the hair salons, on Dearborn and in Wal-Mart, the women thought Newt Gingrich looked like the Pillsbury Doughboy and he didn't have a chance, Ron Paul looked like the little boy with a pot of gold at the end of the rainbow and Mitt Romney was handsome and presidential looking.

There was a consensus among all interviewed that they had enough of Obama and that they would vote for the dog catcher over him.

The most revealing of the findings came from the redneck bars where they didn't care for any of the blokes.

They wanted to draft Gov. Chris Christie of New Jersey. They liked his girth, guts, gumption, grit and gravitas.

The hat boys at the bar even volunteered to reinforce the chairs in the oval office to accommodate him.

MY FRIEND DIED OF ANGST TRYING TO BE WELL

Manasota Key Fl (Storch Report) February 13, 2012 -- We are a nation of wellness, although we are getting fatter by the day. Everyone is trying to help us. The government with Obamacare, the first lady with veggies, forcing nutrition on our children's diet in schools, but when we live beyond expectation, the government plans to cut back on treatment because we have lived beyond usefulness.

The concept to me seems to be duplicitous.

I guess it's about the economy, productivity and what a drug rep once said years ago when he referred to the elderly as 'crocks and crud's".

Duplicity, I like the word, because we see a lot of it today especially from politicians, because it's all about one talking out of both sides of their mouths and often within the same sentence.

I don't know how they do that, but it seems to be more pervasive today.

On one side of the equation the government tries to encourage a healthy life style so you are not a burden to entitlements they provide for you when you are young, because they want you to be beholden to them, and at the same time productive to society.

But once you fall into that part of society of being a 'crock and crud', well, under the system you seem to be expendable, because you are a drain on society, you know, like social security, Medicare, Medicaid and so on. Society didn't ask for it, the liberals wanted to provide it.

But this story is not about a system failure, it is about a system of wellness success.

You see today everything is about an electronic record and medically doctors must adhere to the law when it comes to their patients.

Don't tell your doctor anything you don't want to see on the internet, or for that matter you yourself don't want to read, for it could be deadly.

My friend who I used to meet with frequently for lunch was well up into his 80's.

He appeared to be fit and seemed to follow a healthy lifestyle.

He exercised, maintained his weight, had regular doctor visits, carefully watched his diet and enjoyed life.

One day at lunch he told me how his doctor was modifying his practice, cutting back on his patients and joining one of those concierge practices where his patients would have to join, pay a premium fee per year, and become part of a wellness program. It was so sophisticated that data for his annual physical would be evaluated by the Cleveland Clinic. He kind of thought twice about all this and said, "Wellness in my 80's. I needed it in my 30's."

Nevertheless he told me, "I'm not going to change horses in midstream, even though it's too late for wellness at this stage of my life."

And so the time came for his physical and the wellness program promised.

He completed the exam and it was time for the follow-up visit with his physician and the doctor delivered the good and bad news verbally.

Verbal words are always better than written words, they seem to be softer and you hear what you want to hear.

It wasn't until my friend received the written word from the concierge service and the results from the Cleveland Clinic, on a CD disk that he could carry around in his wallet for emergency; and it wasn't until he printed them out on paper that reality and depression kicked in.

Under the headline of diagnosis it said of my friend: gastro esophageal reflux disease; hypertension and dyslipidemia, renal insufficiency, hypertension cardiovascular disease, carotid disease, low D; elevated MPO; hyperuricemia; degenerative joint disease of the knee; degenerative joint disease of the spine and increased PSA.

Now on top of all of this the doctor recommends further tests to seek out more problems on the basis of these diagnoses.

I received a call from my wife's friend a few months later that my friend had died.

I said what happened? He seemed to be fine. She said he died of angst. I said angst? She said one of the doctor's told her he died of angst over multiple diagnoses of serious diseases, but not one of the diseases killed him.

MICHELLE OBAMA IS NOT AN 'ANGRY BLACK WOMAN'

Washington DC (Storch Report) January 15, 2012 -- It is time to defend first lady Michelle Obama against the charges of being an 'angry black woman,' after all she and her husband President Obama, are part of that elite one percent of the wealthy class of Americans, who Occupy Wall Street are protesting, and it is very difficult to be 'angry' when you're in the same class as half of the members of Congress, who are millionaires.

Show me an angry wealthy person, black or white, and I'll show you a person who is not counting their blessings, and that's not Michelle.

This all came about as a result of a book written by New York Times reporter Jodi Kantor who said there was some kind of tension between the first lady and White House aides serving the president.

Michelle denied this saying people have tried to portray her as "some kind of angry black woman" ever since Barack announced his candidacy for president.

"I guess it's more interesting to imagine this conflicted situation here and a strong woman. I love this job," she asserted.

And I for one believe her, how could one not love a job that comes with the perks that Michelle and her family have enjoyed,

such as the $242,000 vacation she and her daughters, family friends, personal staff and various guests had on a trip to Spain.

Even those that are in that rarified air of the wealthy one percent and born with a silver spoon in their mouth get to stay in a private 3-story villa 5 star luxury hotel at $2,500 a night.

Or, to travel to Spain with family and guests aboard Air Force Two at the cost of $11,351 per hour, using 47,500 gallons of jet fuel with carbon emissions of 1,031 tons of CO2.

But this is okay, because Barack was back home offsetting these costs and carbon emissions by stuffing middle class families into the tiny, but costly, $40,000 Chevy Volt, an electric car that catches fire upon side impact. This move to offset Michelle's Tiffany tastes was about as successful as his Green bailout of solar panel company Solyndra, now in bankruptcy. Chevy has sold a record breaking 7,000 Volts' and is looking to discontinue the line.

Meanwhile Michelle was accompanied by 70 secret service personnel to protect her and her entourage, so they wouldn't have to worry about being accosted by Gypsy's while jaunting around Spain.

Now if this were the only perk, one might begin to understand why Michelle might be an 'angry black woman,' but there was the $2 billion trip to India, several trips to Martha's Vineyard, one of which the family dog, Bo, was flown up privately on a smaller jet, so he could be with the girls, the trip to Africa with the girls and Mom and of course the Christmas vacation in a 7,000 square foot beach house in Hawaii.

Upcoming soon, a ski vacation in Vail.

Now I think you can understand why I don't believe that Michelle Obama is an 'angry black woman,' and is looking for another 4 years of junkets while fighting for the middle class, wealth redistribution and against childhood obesity.

WHEN YOU'RE CLOSER TO THE END THAN THE BEGINNING

Manasota Key FL (Storch Report) January 9, 2012 -- In retrospect life is an evolution of time, places, jobs, careers, and people and when you find yourself closer to the end than the beginning you wonder where it all went and how you got there so fast.

It's a gradual subtle process to get where you are going, some glide through life gracefully while others take the road less traveled and find some detours with bumps along the way.

The first sign that you are distancing yourself from your inception is that you can't physically do what you once could, especially if you were active.

Life is filled with expectations you didn't achieve and you adapt to them as well as the surprises you didn't plan for.

We are less adaptable as we become set in our ways and if we were not adaptable when we were young, we are even more rigid in our ways as we age.

Perhaps that is why we have so many cranky old people in Florida.

You see when you get old, even without any serious illness, your knees hurt, you get lower back pain, the hips falter and the neck has trouble holding up the head.

This happens especially in people that were active when they were young.

Those that were mostly sedentary got a joint pass as they aged and you will find them at The Villages in Florida competing against other former sedentary septuagenarians while the former athletes sit on the sidelines watching with their walkers alongside of them.

No one said life was fair. If you couldn't participate when you were young you can participate when you're old at The Villages, where the competition is less today than what it might have been for them yesterday.

The athletes of yesterday are the fans of today and the fans of yesterday are the competitors of today.

The bones, joints and reflexes of today's competitors do not work as well as they once did and whether a fan or a competitor, it is likely both will meet at the Publix pharmacy picking up a supply of Advil, Aleve, or Tylenol, if not something stronger at the Rx counter.

Someone once said growing old is not for the faint hearted.

NEW YEAR

Manasota Key FL (Storch Report) December 31, 2011 -- Well here it is again, New Year's Eve.

It's that time again to make resolutions for the next year that we don't keep. It's much like those promotional Christmas letters we received in the past weeks that delivered family messages from our friends about the past year and the happenings the way the author saw it, but, perhaps, not the way it really was, that makes the rest of us feel like we are part of a dysfunctional family.

What is it that makes us be dishonest with ourselves? Is that an optimist?

Somehow there are no warts in those annual messages we receive and few people who make those unachievable New Year's resolutions keep them.

It is particularly striking this year when our nation is not fairing too well, that we receive such upbeat messages.

Perhaps I'm living in a zone that my friends are not in. From what I read, I'm beginning to think they are ready to redistribute what they have to others. But I know better.

I see a nation with a record number of housing foreclosures, devalued homes, a record number of unemployed, devalued pension plans, 401 k's, a nation in $15 trillion debt, with little hope to resolve it, other than printing more money, making the Yankee

dollar worth the value of the Euro, and a rudderless nation, once the leader of the free world.

I would like to think there would be social security for my children and grandchildren, after all some are already paying into it, others will be, but there is no guarantee it will be there for them because it is a Ponzi scheme of a grand scale. Some people go to jail for such schemes, but not the US Congress. They created a separate plan for themselves, which they don't steal from.

I guess I'm a pessimist.

I never make a New Year's resolution about anything, therefore I don't have to live up to something I didn't promise myself.

I'm just going to do what I've done before – tell it the way I see it.

I often think of that fun filled flick, "When Harry Met Sally" when they play Auld Lang Syne and Billy Crystal says, "I mean, 'Should old acquaintance be forgot'? Does that mean that we should forget old acquaintances, or does it mean if we happened to forget them, we should remember them, which is not possible because we already forgot?"

Oh, Happy New Year.

OBAMA SHOULD STEP ASIDE FOR THE GOOD OF THE COUNTRY

Manasota Key FL (Storch Report) December 29, 2011 -- **The noble thing for President Obama to do in behalf of the country would be to not run for reelection in 2012.**

Even if he squeaked by, by some miracle, it is unlikely the Democrats would gain control of the House and it is more likely the Republicans will take control of the Senate, making Obama's role untenable, his position dysfunctional, crowning the leader of the free world a titular head.

Obama's Saul Alinsky philosophy hasn't been addressed much since he was a candidate, although GOP candidate Newt Gingrich raised it yesterday during an interview with NBC . . . the Marxist thesis and its big government, entitlement policies have failed the president.

It is time that Obama recognize that America trends to the right of center and that he and the left wing Alinsky philosophy is out of step with what this nation believes and stands for.

Robert Reich, the former Labor Secretary under President Bill Clinton, predicts that Obama will swap his VP Joe Biden for Secretary of State Hillary Clinton, to win reelection.

It is not so far-fetched an idea for the Chicago Pol Obama, where, with that kind of upbringing, they do anything to win.

It would work for both Obama and Clinton; Barack could fuel his ego for a second term, travel, go on vacation to Hawaii and play golf while Hillary could work towards a run for the presidency in four years.

With a GOP controlled congress, we could name POTUS King, and the VEEP Queen, at least that would fulfill one of Obama's goals – to make America more like Europe.

CHRISTMAS LETTERS

Manasota Key FL (Storch Report) December 3, 2011 -- Yes, it's that time of year again when I receive those Christmas letters from my septuagenarian friends telling me how they are repelling skyscraper's in New York after completing the iron man contest in Hawaii.

They make me feel so good that each year I mean to write them and tell them how much the letters pick me up especially after I return from my physical therapist and completing my back exercises which allows me to put one foot in front of the other to make it to my car.

However, I just don't seem to get around to writing them. In fact I don't know if they would have the time to read my letter because they are so busy traveling.

And when they travel to Paris, Italy, Germany and Switzerland they are climbing mountains, they even manage to find mountains to climb in underground caves.

They walk the Great Wall in China, ride camels in Egypt, scuba dive in the Seychelles and take pictures of themselves and lions on safari.

When they take pictures they make sure the subject is so far away you can't see the wrinkles on their faces.

Mid-way through the letter I am so breathless I take a break and watch TV – the Travel Channel – to see what they have seen and I've been missing. I've been thinking of writing them a Christmas Letter to tell them what I've seen on TV.

The best part of these letters is when they get to tell me about their children and grandchildren. Oh, Bristol is a prosecutor in LA, Michael is a brain surgeon at Georgetown and Buffy is a TV Anchor with Fox News. Oh, and my 12-year-old granddaughter Bethany is a nationally ranked tennis player.

The last time I was ranked was after walking away from the hos d'oeuvre table after eating Pout l'Evegue, a 13th century French cheese ranked the slinkiest cheese in the world.

I have to go to the 'Y' now, and jump off the repelling wall.

IF IT'S STONE CRAB SEASON IN FLORIDA, CAN THE SNOW BIRDS BE FAR BEHIND?

Manasota Key Fl (Storch Report) November 14, 2011 -- The Snow Birds are already arriving early, I guess that fall Nor'easter snow storm chased them South earlier than expected – I just hope they leave their migrating drunken Robin's home this year.

The Robin is fond of the berries on our Cabbage Palms, consume them and fly drunkenly into our windows and do some unmentionable things around our pool as they quench their dehydration from their alcohol consumption.

Oh, stone crabs they are a delicacy here in South Florida, and a pricy treat.

The season just opened and the medium, large and jumbo stone crabs are looking good and their prices are matching their good looks.

I don't know how much you know about the harvesting of these crustaceans but the fishing industry doesn't kill them they just crack off one claw, throw them back into the sea and they grow another claw for another human feast or by some other predator.

Stone crabs feed on oysters and other crustaceans, their predators are horse conchs, grouper, sea turtles, cobia, octopuses, and of course humans.

It's a good feeling to eat stone crabs, because the crustacean does not die. They lose their claws easily to escape from predators. The larger of the two claws is the 'crusher claw' the smaller one is the 'pincer claw'. If the larger claw is on the right, the crab is right handed and this is good to know when eating stone crabs, and I don't exactly know why other than its larger. And, that's a good thing.

When I think about it, I'll bet the Robin wishes he/she could grow another liver, following their drunken migration binge to Florida's Cabbage Palms.

Oh, the price of stone crabs? This year mediums are running about $16 a pound, large about $23 a pound and jumbos, forget-about-it. I think this may be a Jersey term – but please leave the Robins up there.

Now, the prices I am quoting are from Publix and a local fish stand, not a restaurant. You can bump these prices up a few notches if you are eating out.

We had a real treat the other night, my wife brought home a half pound of medium stone crabs from Publix, and she paid $8 – she's from the Mid-West. That afternoon I went to a local fish shack and bought another pound of large stone crabs for $20 – but I'm from the East.

We OD'd on stone crabs that evening and had a feast. I think it's worth paying the higher price for the larger stone crab rather than trying to do a root canal on a shell.

Now, this report is coming from the Southwest coast of Florida, but stone crabs have, I believe, a much more storied history on the East Coast of Florida.

I think it had something to do with Joe Fischer who started a fish shack business in Miami back in 1913. But it wasn't until 1921 that Joe's partner James Allison, who was interested in marine research, invited a Harvard ichthyologist – I wonder who his predators were – to Miami to do some research.

The researcher brought in a burlap sack of stone crabs, they figured out how to serve them – broiled, cracked, with hash brown potatoes, Cole slaw and mayonnaise and they were an instant success. "We hit the jackpot with that one," the descendants gloat today. They charged 75 cents for 4 or 5 stone crabs, 25 cents for potatoes and 25 cents for an order of Cole slaw.

Today Joe's Stone Crabs in Miami is an institution. You can order a dinner for two in season by mail if you are not in Miami; however, the prices are not quite the same: dinner for two, medium, $276.95; selects, $305.95; large, $328.95.

Oh, I didn't want you think I forgot about the Snow Birds. Florida has always welcomed them, the Yankee, Canadian, Mid-Western, Western dollar as well as the foreign whatever, especially in these times.

However, as a resident of the dangling chad state, I will continue to welcome them, but resent them from overcrowding my favorite restaurants, roads and forcing me to drive my shopping cart and car defensively.

PORK & CHEESE GIN FLAMBÉ, A GOURMET DELIGHT

Manasota Key FL (Storch Report) October 27, 2011 -- I was rummaging through some memorabilia the other day – a metaphor for cleaning out – and found a menu I wrote in a previous life with a previous wife. It all came about because we belonged to a group that met annually for a black or white tie New Year's Eve dinner created collectively by the group and held in each other's homes. There was a pre planning cocktail party to select a menu, assign who would do what and then of course the main event. I wrote the menu and on the back page I did a column, not too different than what I do today, and the menu I found was the 5th annual meeting of the group. I selected to do a satirical piece that year and here it is, circa December 31, 1975:

Each year I like to think that on this page I discuss a topic that is provocative philosophical and titillating. This year, I have selected to forgo being provocative and philosophical to share with you a recent gastronomic delight that I had the pleasure of experiencing.

One evening I came home to find a note from the one who does the cooking in our house, "Gone shopping with the kids . . . make dinner for yourself."

Now there are times when I have the urge for something special rather than something simple, and it was on one of those occasions that I rose to the challenge and prepared a superb dinner that would be cherished by the most discriminating epicurean palate.

The meal opened with a 1975 Balish (a local liquor store) gin and Canada Dry tonic topped off with a twist of A&P lemon rind. The mixture of gin to tonic was judicious and the cocktail proved to have admirable character.

To properly create the balance of tastes, I followed with a pate de fruites de dry roasted nuts of Planters, prepared according to my own recipe.

A half inch layer of creamy-style peanut butter was troweled onto a Ritz cracker, then half an apple was crudely diced and pressed firmly into the peanut butter interspersed with five dry roasted nuts halved.

The apples and the gin and tonic seemed to help keep the peanut butter from becoming cemented to the palate.

I followed with a dish that added up to a certain rapture – a croustade of hard boiled chicken eggs, carefully sprinkling a pinch of salt between each bite. The dish was particularly good and notably colorful due to the fact I was using left over Easter eggs.

The blue and red dyes had seeped through the shell onto the white of the egg and colorfully intermingled with the yolk.

This delicacy was accompanied by a refrigerated stein of Budweiser beer, 1975, Newark.

At this point, the stomach was ready for serious eating and while getting ready to prepare it I began to sip on my second gin and tonic, Balish 1975.

I turned up the electric range to 500 degrees, placed an oversize pat of butter in a skillet and began to fill the air with the smell of burning butter.

I then unwrapped the Taylor pork roll cut the edges one eighth of an inch apart and placed two pieces in the dangerously hot skillet.

The kitchen was filled with instant smoke that caused the eyes to smart. I then placed a single slice of Kraft's individually wrapped yellow sandwich cheese on the top of each pork roll and flamed same in Balish gin, 1975.

It was at this point that I came close to using for the first time the fire extinguisher that is on the wall of the stairwell to the recreation room. However, the flames remained under control and the pork and cheese became respectively charred and melted as desired.

In the meantime I toasted two slices of air-filled bread, scraped the pork and cheese from the grease-filled pan and placed each slice on the toast.

By separately toasting the bread and the pork and cheese I was able to maintain the dryness of the main course which was further aided by a selection of greasy Wise potato chips.

For my salad I chose a fine contrast of old lettuce slightly browned on the edges and topped with diced celery and Kraft oil and vinegar dressing. For the wine I selected a 1974 Mogen David Beaujolais, flavored with three pickled martini onions.

It too had a very distinctive and admirable character. It was again necessary to clear the palate, and for my fruit course I prepared tinned Del Monte fruit cup clotted with sour cream.

At last it was time for the dish the entire meal had been building toward – dessert.

I prepared bananas gin flambé. I took one ripe banana, peeled and sliced lengthwise, cut the skin in triangles, placed same in a flat chafing dish, added two tablespoons of brown sugar, one tablespoon of butter, a dash of cinnamon, one large scoop of vanilla ice cream, and to maintain consistency poured Balish gin, 1975, overall and flamed. I could not believe the taste buds . . . it was a sublime creation.

To again clear the palate I concluded with a gin and tonic, Balish 1975, followed by a half a glass of chilled Briocachi. It was truly superb.

—

Author's note: We were serious adults in those years trying to make our way in life and all were trying to succeed during the times

and provide for our families. In another section of the menu, I did conclude with a piece of philosophy and quoted Arnold J. Toynbee. I now find how ironic, timely and poignant that it was then and particularly so today: "The World's greatest need . . . is mutual confidence. No human being ever knows all the secrets of another's heart. Yet there is enough confidence between mother and child, husband and wife, buyer and seller . . . to make social life a practical possibility. Confidence may be risky, but it is nothing as risky as mistrust."

OBAMA NEVER LET'S A GOOD SPEAKING VENUE GO TO WASTE

Manasota Key Fl (Storch Report) September 21, 2011 -- President Obama gave three speeches in one at the UN today.

He told those listening that the world was doing fine since he became president and that's why he is drawing down troops in Iraq and Afghanistan, that democracy was coming to Egypt and Libya, things were improving in South Africa and the Taliban was on the run since he ordered the killing of Osama bin Laden.

He then told Israel and Palestine to walk in each other's moccasins and said five times that achieving peace was hard work, as though the audience didn't hear him the first time.

Then he wrapped up his third speech with a grab bag of domestic issues, but noted that this global world was attached at the hip making reference to the economy and in passing noting some bad luck with natural disasters.

I hope his dwindling progressive base was listening or at least being roused, because it has been at least 24 hours since they last heard from him.

THE EMMYS – IF YOU WANT AN ACCURATE REPORT OF WHAT HAPPENED, LOOK SOMEWHERE ELSE

Los Angeles (Storch Report) September 18, 2011 -- The Emmys, hosted by a gay girl that looks like Ellen, filled with double and triple 'wows', 'Oh, My Gods' and 'I'm from Illinois' from those accepting awards, with an over use of video tapes for a live performance left me wanting to go home with Betty White who the host Jane Lynch said, was "the only reason we started the show at 5PM."

What ever happened to Billy Chrystal who knew how to tell a joke understood what a segue was and was as good as Robert De Niro told him in Analyze This and That, "You, You, are Good."

I really don't care to watch a live show and see the opening moments belabored with a series of videotape performances before the host appears live in the first of two ugly dresses.

Oh, and then there was the cleavage to the navel holding in small boobs and the recipient wondering what she was going, 'to tell her therapists,' after winning the award?

There was again the crying, you would think after all these years of acting they would be able to control that, and poor jokes about what their Dad might think of the make-up they have to wear, like I look like a 'female harlot.'

And, how about the writers who write funny lines for others, win an award for themselves, but can't write themselves a funny line.

Oh and Jane Lynch delivered her second funny line, "I was our next presenter's therapist", and she introduced Charlie Sheen. She also said, "Many people are curious as to why I'm a Lesbian . . ." I wasn't curious, why does she think so many others are?

And there was a winner that used the words, "Holly Smokes", I thought for a moment Phil Rizzuto was hosting.

Jane Lynch showed up in her second dress of the night – it was as ugly as her first and those Emmytone singers couldn't hold a tune to the Andrews Sisters.

Kate Winslet appeared on the red carpet looking dazzling in her red gown, svelte figure and breasts from the portrait in the Titanic. She played alongside of Leonardo DiCaprio, who played Jack Dawson in Titanic. But the actual drawing was done by James Cameron. By the way, Kate won an Emmy tonight as the lead actress in a mini-series as Mildred Pierce on HBO, and you can take that fact home to the bank.

Then there was Sofia Vergara of Modern Family, a Columbia bombshell that also appeared on the red carpet in an equally red dress with an accent that nobody notices.

I have trouble catching up with these sitcoms that I guess they were honoring tonight; after all, I'm just beginning to enjoy Cheers and Becker on the Reelz Channel.

ANTS WOULD DO A BETTER JOB

Washington DC (Storch Report) July 25, 2011 -- Little did I know, until discovering a feature on CBS's Sunday Morning, that cutter ants from Belize could do a better job of resolving the debt ceiling debt reduction crisis than the lackluster leadership of the Obama administration and the Congress collectively.

It turns out that humans are too smart for the functioning of a whole society. In other words it makes some sense to be stupid because it's better for the society as a whole.

Human behavior comes into play and as it turns out we have a lot to learn about this from the ant.

You see in the ant colony nobody is in charge, no bureaucrats, no foreman or managers, presidents, speakers – nobody telling anybody what to do.

I'll bet you're getting the picture now when it comes to Boehner, McConnell, Reid, Pelosi and Obama.

Now, I don't know what you know about those pesty little things under our feet, but there is a whole world down there and they operate without currency, leaders and they feed millions in a very organized manner.

The cutter ant in Belize operates much like a can opener. They march off much like soldiers to trees where they cut out a can-like top of a leaf and carry it back to their colony. Often other ants

catch a ride back home on the leaf, the early version of what is known today as carpooling.

Those that study these ants call it conserving energy, but it looks more like malingering to me.

These ants don't eat the leaves, they farm them by burying the leaf and turning them into mulch on which they raise a fungus, because they are fungus eating ants which produces ambrosia.

Ants create underground cities and highways and operate in assembly lines. They are not very smart individually, but as colonies they are quite intelligent. There are soldiers, nurses, sanitation specialists, highway construction workers and even 'suicide bomber' ants.

They say these ancient ants are much like the terrorists of today. They just walk up to the enemy and explode spraying a toxic yellow glue over itself and everything around it.

Most of an ant colony is made up of females. The male impregnates the female then dies and then she just lays eggs.

Perhaps there is something to be learned here, you see because the females survive and thrive together, all without a leader which would be very hard for our politicians of today to understand.

Little did passengers who fly Southwest Airlines know that they board a plane the way in which ants would?

Doug Lawson, a systems analyst at Southwest, was asked by the airline to help figure out the most efficient way to help get passengers on a plane and apparently the first thing he thought of was an ant colony.

He said he thought of this because ants 'do complicated things with very simple rules."

So he used mathematically-modeled ants to determine the most efficient way of boarding a plane which turns out to be open seating.

Lawson said that, "when he simulated what the different airlines are doing, it turns out that with assigned seats there's a one-third chance that you're going to ask two people to get up, whereas

open seating – since the middle seat is the undesirable one – generally that's the one that's last to be filled, so only one person is likely to get up, the person sitting near the aisle."

Lawson said that, for human behavior, ants have a lot to teach us about activities that don't require a lot of brain power." Perhaps that's our problem in Washington DC. Ant colonies have very specific tasks and that's how the ant society is which has evolved over millions of years, according to Lawson.

According to Mark Moffett- a biologist, author, photographer and ant-enthusiast – "Arguably, humans are too smart for the functioning of the whole society, it pays to be individually stupid."

And all this time I thought what was going on in Washington was the other way around. Thank you CBS for the enlightenment, now the markets are trying to understand why the politicians in DC don't operate more like ants.

TODAY WAS ALL ABOUT PEAS, LIGHT BULBS & THE DEFICIT

Washington DC (Storch Report) July 11, 2011 -- For those who could never change a light bulb, help is on the way and for those that didn't like to eat their peas, President Obama told us today we must eat them to help with the deficit.

The government will help you by enforcing upon the public a new light bulb that will last longer, provide less light to read by, cost significantly more, will be hazardous to your health, be more difficult to dispose of, but you will be afforded the benefit to change light bulbs fewer times.

This will allow you to go to remedial light bulb changing school in the interim.

Now as for peas, we must 'eat our peas', President Obama said today. We need to do this to help with the deficit.

I mean after all, this President has 'bent over backwards' to meet with Republicans and all Republican Speaker of the House John Boehner is looking for is a dance; because he said today, 'it takes two to Tango.'

The metaphors are flying high and wide.

Big government is in play. I just hope Michelle Obama doesn't have any peas planted in her victory garden behind the White House.

The government is so intrusive today that even Obama has to sneak out of the White House with some buddies for a cheese burger and then sneaks some more back for the staff as a treat.

Meanwhile, Michelle is trying to prevent kids from having a burger, or soda pop in school, salt is being taken out of restaurants, the government is telling us what cars to drive and what our BMI should be.

Oh, and cigarettes, I wonder how Obama is doing with that habit?

I never tried a cigarette, therefore I don't have much compassion for those with the habit, especially with the evidence that has been available for a long time that it is a health hazard for the smoker and those exposed to passive smoke.

If the product is so bad, it shouldn't be on the market. Isn't that much like the light bulb?

I think the cigarette is worse than Edison's light bulb. I would pick the latter to have in my household rather than the former.

They are debating it today in Congress to get the stupid new bulb out of some environmental bill that was signed by George Bush as part of a larger package and it was slipped into the bill by no other than Nancy Pelosi, who probably has stock in GE. The vote is going to take place tomorrow.

Now, as for veggies, I am not a fan of them and on the basis of what Obama said today, perhaps he isn't either; for he portrayed eating peas as a penalty to passing the debt deficit ceiling.

The intrusiveness of this government is preventing me at this late stage of my life from meeting a goal I always wanted to achieve, changing a light bulb of my choice in my own house.

A DYSFUNCTIONAL WORLD

Manasota Key Fl (Storch Report) July 8, 2011 -- When using the word dysfunctional we often associate it with 'family', why isn't it more often associated with the word 'world', because that's the global environment in which we live?

And, wouldn't it be logical to think that if you lived in a dysfunctional 'world' that this dysfunction would trickle down to 'family'?

In my opinion I think we have a dysfunctional President, who apparently came from a dysfunctional 'family'. And somehow this seems to be a juxtaposition to the point I am trying to make!

And now he is on his way to creating a dysfunctional nation and plans to put us all on Ritalin for ADHD, but will refuse to pay for the medication under Obamacare.

Perhaps it's a chicken and egg thing?

The world is in dire straits, but I can't figure out whether it came from the bottom up, or the top down.

Look what's happening in Greece, I mean after all, this is an ancient country and society with all kinds of ancient knowledge. But they are in bankruptcy, as we in the US are on the verge of, and I wonder could it be all about the entitlements they have become used to?

Perhaps it's all about Obama's concept of wealth redistribution evolving from all those great Greek philosophers?

You know, I get confused and feel a bit like Colombo, you know that late detective, Peter Falk, who always had one more question.

He played dumb but we all knew he was smart until he said a dumb thing.

I mean how do I deal with all this dysfunction and also understand Chavez of Venezuela, the Castro's of Cuba, Ahmadinejad of Iran, Lee Myung-Bak of South Korea or for that matter Islam, Muslims and terrorists and Obama's rational for all these wars?

I tried calling Colombo, but he didn't answer his phone.

WORDS OBAMA SHOULD AVOID USING BETWEEN NOW AND 2012 . . .

Washington DC (Storch Report) June 10, 2011 -- We are now two-and-a-half years into the first term of President Obama's administration and a lot has happened, and I would be the last one to make judgments on whether it has been a good or bad start. I would rather leave that call up to the voters. However, I thought I might pass along some words and sentences to the president he might consider avoiding between now and 2012 – that is if he wants to be reelected:

"At the outset, I'd like to make it clear that I have made terrible mistakes that have hurt the people I care about . . . and I'm deeply sorry."

"I have not been honest with myself, the people or the media . . ."

"I am so sorry to have disrupted life in this way . . ."

"But, let us not forget, I inherited this mess and I did not make it worse . . . nevertheless, I'm sorry . . ."

"I campaigned as an anti-war candidate and we are now into four wars, I'm looking for a fifth and that should put a nail in the coffin of this nation . . . it was a hugely regrettable mistake, and I'm sorry."

"I can't say with certitude that we won't have a double dip recession, or for that matter an Obama depression, and I'm sorry."

"I take full responsibility for my actions."

"I promised you transparency, but I am going to take this columnists' advice and avoid saying these words from now on, I'm sorry."

SALES OF WEINER'S GOING UP . . . COULD BE?

Washington DC (Storch Report) June 2, 2011 -- I'll bet Oscar Mayer wish they thought of this promotion, perhaps Fruit of the Loom too!

I don't think much of hot dogs, franks, Weiner's (wiener's) or dogs (dawg's) Nathan's or for that matter dachshunds unless I'm at the ballpark.

But the Weiner is on everybody's lip's these days in the halls of Congress.

However, I don't think there are too many singing the song, "I'd Love To Be An Oscar Mayer Weiner" in these hallow halls these days, least of all Rep. Anthony Weiner, (D, NY) who is all caught up in his shorts over a crotch shot that was twittered and he can't say with 'certitude' whether the photo in gray underpants was his.

The press asked Weiner every which way whether the crotch shot was his, but he said he couldn't say with 'certitude' that it wasn't. But they failed to ask him if he had gray undershorts.

He would not say whether he took the picture or not, but denied he sent the image to Gennette Nicole Cordova, a 21 year-old journalism student who received it via Twitter,

"I was hacked, it was a trickster, a prank, mischief," he said.

Someone called it a 'slight thing' during a TV interview. Perhaps it is.

Nevertheless Weiner became visibly testy and combative when pressed on the issue yesterday, but today invited the media in for more interviews to give the story legs.

I never knew how many hot dogs were sold in America. My research shows that this year alone, 23 million hot dogs will be sold in major league ballparks, that's enough weiners to stretch coast to coast from Dodger's Stadium in Los Angeles to Camden Yards in Baltimore and that's quite a stimulus program.

As a result of Weinergate I think these sales will get an additional boost of a Viagra sort. This is certainly on the way to stimulating the economy and jobs.

Now how can we get a gray pair of Fruit of the Looms in on this promotion?

Weiner spent the day trying to boost sales for his product which is already expected to represent 1.06 million more Weiner's sold in 2010. With the advent of the Weiner Dog, even if they have to make a slight adjustment in the spelling of the name – after all it means the same thing – there should be soaring Fruit of the Loom gray underwear sales throughout the nation.

"When you're named Weiner, it kind of goes with the territory," he told CNN, adding that a hacker may have accessed his account just to make a joke of his name.

Weiner was known on the hill as a bachelor playboy, before he married Huma Abedin, an aide to Secretary Hillary Clinton.

As I see it, Weiner was one of the few Democrats to stimulate the economy, increase sales in an industry, and possibly two, that will undoubtedly sell more Weiner's which will result in more jobs in the American hot dog industry.

Take me out to the ball game!

ROYALS BRING OUT THE PROPER AND IMPROPER TOPPERS

London (Storch Report) April 30, 2011 -- For the ladies privy to being invited to the Royals marriage of the century one article was the derigeur: Fascinators.

It really does take the Brits to come up with the word fascinators and of course the hat to accompany the word, because these are the people that traditionally don't know enough to get out of the noon day sun.

Now the topper that the Queen wore to the Disney performance of 'Kiss Me (again) Kate' could be called a proper topper. After all what else could it be, even if the rest of the outfit, as one American comic said, looked like a school bus?

Then there were those that pranced like peacocks with rudimentary plumage sprouting from a barrette and others wearing crowns that proved to be nose pointers.

I always liked hats, in fact my mother used to call me the mad hatter. However, most of the hats I wore were baseball hats. I probably have more hats today than Imelda Marcos had shoes.

Most of my hats are traditional, Indiana Jones hats, captain's hats, sailing hats, golf hats, safari hats, Aussie hats and pith helmets. I only have one crazy or fascinator hat, it's one with grey hair for my shaved head.

Hats are important for me whether I'm in the tropics or elsewhere.

Everyone attending the Royal wedding was provided with a 22 page book of etiquette on how to behave and what to wear. For example, men were to wear a dress uniform, with sword, as the cad, Prince Charles and his father, the stiff, Prince Philip did. The morning suit that Sir Elton John and his significant other wore was smashing. Those in a business suit, known in the UK as a lounge suit, were boring on a scale of one to 10 and were duly noted by the Queen.

There were many women wearing feathers from their coffers and I was surprised not to see more birds nesting; and of course there were the flying saucers some on top of the head and others off to the side so they could get a peck on the cheek that is if they didn't have lift off before the event.

I don't exactly know how to explain this topper, but it sure does make a lady tall. For me a hat on a lady is a distraction, I'm just not looking at the usual assets that I am pleased by.

However, there was one class act that stole the show and it wasn't the bride. It was Pippa, the 27-year-old sister of the bride who proved to be an Ass . . . set to the spectacle, not a fascinating distraction.

KATE & WILLIAM GOT MARRIED, AND I WATCHED FROM ACROSS THE POND

London (Storch Report) April 29, 2011 -- Yes it's 4 AM EST in the US 9AM in London, partly cloudy, 55 degrees and I am up and about to deliver this message to you, because I am sure you wanted to know what I had to say about the Royal spectacle of a Prince marrying a Commoner.

Prince William now prefers that his new wife be called Princess Catherine disposing of her Commoner label. The official logo on programs and precious take-away gifts for guests is C&W, after all this was a no brainier to Royal advisers, for CW juxtaposed would be WC and in the UK, that's a Water Closet.

Oh, how properly British and after all no one has ever been known to call Westminster Abby a John.

Royal weddings in the United States are looked upon for their entertainment value, much like American Idol and Dancing with the Stars.

A CNN poll showed that more in the US would be catching their zz's rather than witnessing the pomp and circumstance of a Royal wedding that would exceed the fantasy of a Walt Disney flick.

Ho hum, I guess that's why I'm here watching this stuff across the pond.

Kate Middleton, the commoner and Princess to be is from Buckle bury. I don't know where that is, but if I were from there I wouldn't admit it. She had an Uncle that was a drug addict and an Aunt who was a stripper.

She likes to frequent a pub called the Pigs Ear in London, I like to frequent a pub in Rotunda Fl. called the Pig & Whistle.

I guess we have something in common as commoners

She went to St Andrews College, where Prince William Mountbatten Windsor went, some say she did this to catch a King to-be and as the story goes he became smitten with her when she partook in a fashion show in a see-through dress and apparently the Prince liked what he saw.

They lived together for eight years, with a brief parting in 2007, but reunited. She studied art history, he geography. Prince William is an RAF search and rescue helicopter pilot and she a commoner/ Princess.

Her parents have a thriving party favor business, her mother was an airline attendant.

Kate's 29 and time to be bedded for heirs to the Monarchy.

The wedding will cost $100 million, 1 million showed up for the fantasy wedding, 2 1/2 million watched on TV and the drama is expected to return a billion to the UK economy, which is in a recession.

This is but another chapter in the Royals longest running soap opera, a national celebration for the future King and Queen.

President Obama and his wife Michelle were not invited to the spectacle, which should give Whoopi Goldberg, of 'The View', another opportunity to call the 'race card.'

Here's what I think I saw of the celebration through my sleepy eyes: There were lots of hats, enough to put the Easter parade down Fifth Avenue in New York to shame, designer dresses, cleavage and a spit shine on the streets of London with enough flowers and pollen to cause one to pop a Claritin.

Sir Elton John and his significant other filed in, in tails and a morning coat and a purple tie to cheers from the crowds waving and acknowledging the national treasure he is to the Brits.

UK flags adorned light poles as the Royal Guard marched down the streets to the Abby followed by limos and buses with not a speck of dust anywhere to be seen.

The Middleton family were seated up front on the left, the late Princess Diana's family, the Spencer's were seated behind them, and Prince William's Royals were seated up front to the right.

Although this was not a State event because Prince William is not a direct heir to the throne, it had all the pomp and circumstance of one. After all, a 22 page etiquette book was issued to guests so they knew how to dress and behave.

Prince William and his brother arrived together, William in a red Colonel's military uniform of the Irish Guard with a blue tunic, Harry in a blue military uniform of the Royal Garter with a red tunic riding in a maroon Rolls Royce adorned with the Royal crest on the roof.

The Abby's bells rang as the brothers arrived, white gloves giving that special short Royal wave to the crowds.

Most of the women wore hats looking more like flying saucers attached to one side of the head covering the face.

The other popular hat was one that sat on the top of the head looking much like a bird's nest.

Prince Charles, the cad, arrived with Camellia looking as stiff as his father.

Queenie arrived in one of her traditional hats all decked out in a symphony of yellow.

Then it was time for Kate to appear wearing a Tiara, veil and long train looking quite elegant but waving like the commoner she is. The wave will stiffen with time, perhaps as quickly as she becomes a Princess.

Everything came off on time, you wouldn't expect anything else, even the sun popped out as the Princess to be entered the Abby.

And so it was, a stunning ceremony amidst flourishing trumpets, songs, prayers, impeccably timed that the smiling, elegant bride Kate, now with a more regal wave, became Princess Catherine

wife of Prince William riding off to Buckingham Palace into the London fog as millions of Brits cheered the newlyweds, waiting for the famous kiss on the balcony of the Palace.

For the bride a simple 'I will' transformed commoner Kate, to Princess Catherine, Duchess of Cambridge.

CAN OUR LEADERS OF TODAY TELL THE GOOD GUYS FROM THE BAD?

Washington DC (Storch Report) March 30,2011 -- It was easier yesterday, the Indians were the bad guys and the cowboys were the good guys, but then came along the Lone Ranger and Tonto and that was confusing; until a tribe of Indians attacked both and the Lone Ranger said to Tonto, "What are we going to do now kimosabe?" And Tonto said, Whata ya mean "we."

The sheriff was good and Jessie James was bad; but Robin Hood was bad yesterday, but perhaps good today, because he practiced wealth re-distribution.

In World War II the bad guys had oriental eyes and their allies had hob nail boots.

It seemed in those days you could always tell the good guys from the bad guys by what they wore.

Often in a war the combatants could tell who the bad guy was by the uniform he was wearing.

And, those sitting on the sidelines could tell who to root for depending on what side they were on.

Since 9/11 the US has taken the battle for that atrocity, one that was greater than what brought this country into World War II, to the Middle East and started three wars with three different countries.

And, I still don't know if we know who the good guys are.

In the Middle East you can't tell the good guys from the bad guys, because they all wear sheets and look like towel heads.

An American spy stands out like a sore thumb.

President Obama calls our bombardment of Libya a humanitarian cause to protect the civilians, but from a policy position he thinks Qaddafi must go, but he's not a target.

He promises no "American boots on the ground," but signs a secret order allowing "covert operations." That I guess, means that the CIA is trying to find out the good guys from the bad ones. And because Obama said no "boots on the ground" they are wearing flip flops.

The NATO Commander, an Admiral in The United States Navy, Adm James G. Stavridis warns that the rebels in Libya have Al-Qaeda links.

Meanwhile, Secretary of State Hillary Clinton gets caught between a rock and a hard place when the Obama administration takes a position that the UN arms embargo on Libya does not prohibit countries from providing arms to rebels who are fighting to over throw the Qaddafi regime.

Clinton said yesterday that no "decision" has been made to provide arms to the rebels, but others say it is under active consideration. Are they the good guys?

Now they say Sen. John Kerry (D-Mass) has evolved as the Obama administration's key interlocutor, (wow, I'll have to look that one up) with Syrian president Bashar al Assad.

Kerry has promoted the view that 'engagement' between the US and Syria could change the orientation of a regime that has been Iran's closest Arab ally, and a weapons supplier to Hezbollah in Lebanon and Hamas in the Gaza Strip.

Does Kerry really know whether he's a good guy or a bad guy? I don't think so, two weeks ago mass protests erupted because of Assad's brutal repressions. To date Assad's security forces slaughtered 60 people for taking to the streets to shout slogans such as "we want only freedom" and "no to Iran."

I don't know about you, but I don't think our leaders have any idea who the good guys are when it seems to me they are about to support the bad guys.

Bring back the Indians, they weren't so bad. We didn't know it at the time, but we screwed them anyway.

OBAMA'S WAR IN LIBYA, A 'KINETIC MILITARY ACTION'

Washington DC (Storch Report) March 25, 2011 -- It is now clear, the brain trust within the Obama administration spent more time working on euphemisms for the word 'war' against Libya then they did defining the coalition's military mission, goal or end game.

According to reliable sources it was the President that came up with the idea to form a task force to search for another word other than war to explain his military action.

After all he wasn't going to consult with Congress before he and his coalition were going to war with Libya. They were going to take their cue from UN resolution 1973, declare war and then Obama was going to Rio.

According to our reliable sources Obama met with his close advisers, told them to form a secret task force so that when he got back from vacation, the White House could explain the military action to Congress and the people.

Obama made note that he didn't want to use any words previous administrations used when they went to war. He said, "You know like hostilities, police action or conflict." He told his advisers that it might be helpful if members of the task force, "we're good at Scrabble."

A name was given to this highly secret committee: "The Verbal Aerobics Task Force" (VATF). Obama told his advisers that if the task force does a good job, it could be a permanent committee to work on other 'word smith' problems the White House might have.

Obama went on vacation and the task force had a week to complete its assignment.

Our source, who spoke on anonymity would not reveal the names of the members of the committee, but said the group went back to medieval times to come up with the answer.

"You see, back in medieval times they had non-orbital bombardments with kinetic projectiles such as lobbing stones with devices like catapults or trebuchets, but you see even in those days this was considered, "siege warfare".

He went on to say that "warfare" of course would be verboten to the task force's assignment.

But then, according to our source, they came up with kinetic bombardment which is a si-fi term that evolved out of the 'cold war' and according to Wikipedia it's the act of attacking a planetary surface with an inert projectile, where the destructive force comes from kinetic energy of the projectile impacting at very high velocities.

Eureka, the top Scrabble player on the task force got it: "Kinetic Military Action."

And according to my source, KMA could go down in the annals of military history, "because war has lost its meaning."

Apparently the task force member who got the word Kinetic, asked for his 11 points.

TAKE HIM OUT I CAN'T GET THE SPELLING OF HIS NAME RIGHT

Washington DC (Storch Report) March 21, 2011 -- There's a lot of alphabet soup being used in the spelling of an ugly man's name, who resurfaced again in the news in recent weeks.

And, I'll bet President Barack Hussein Obama, wishes he never heard of his name even though he's been around longer than Obama's been alive and is wondering why someone else didn't take out this man long before journalists had trouble spelling it, and he had to deal with it.

Blame it on Bush.

But, my personal dilemma is that I have spelled Moammar Gadhafi every which way to Sunday, and I don't know what the hell that means.

In reviewing my reports I know I spelled it Gadhafi and Qaddafi, I never misspelled Moammar because I didn't use it, until maybe this time and according to some of the spelling I misspelled it as well.

Apparently his name is easier to say than to spell, especially after reviewing what's happened in the spelling of his name on the Internet and in major newspapers across the land.

The New York Times says he is Col. Muammar el-Qaddafi.

The Wall Street Journal and AP says he's Moammar Gadhafi.

Reuters says Muammar Gaddafi and the LA Times goes with Moammar Kaddafi.

Wikipedia uses Muammar al-Gaddafi.

Google says in order of hits its Wikipedia in a landslide:

- **Muammar al-Gaddafi 1.05 million hits**
- **Moammar Gadhafi 175,000 hits**
- **Muammar el-Qaddafi 57,900 hits**
- **Moammar Kadafi 9,340 hits**

I think I'm going to go with Dictator Gadhafi, but I wish the coalition forces would take him out before I have to spell his name again, because any spelling of his name comes out BAD.

SUPER BOWL XLV, A POTPOURRI OF IMPEDIMENTA, AND, OH, THE GAME

Manasota Key FL (Storch Report) February 6, 2011 -- It was just too much from tailgate, to the Obama interview, to pre-game, to post game with, a barrage of intermittent commercials to remember whether I saw the Super Bowl.

I do remember Christina Aguilera singing a terrible version of the National Anthem, to which she couldn't remember the words, while looking somewhat like Adam Sandler in an earlier Tailgate skit with Jenifer Aniston, where he wore a wig similar to the hair style of Aguilera.

Lea Michele did a beautiful job with America the Beautiful.

Then for further distractions there was President George Bush and Laura in a special Dallas Cowboy box with John Madden on one side, texting, and NY Yankees A-Rod being fed popcorn by Penelope Cruz on the other.

There was a lot of stuff going on. During the pre-game, they threw me Bill O'Reilly with an exclusive interview with President Obama, who declared before my very eyes that he was not for wealth redistribution. If that is not the case why do all of his policies reflect it? For a moment I thought I was hearing messages from another planet. But no there was more, he said (Obama) that he was confident in changes for Egypt.

Now this was a lot to digest with my Cuban sandwich and gin and tonic.

But then there was this Pepsi Max Ad with zero calories and some kind of a torpedo cooler which shoots out cans, that hits a guy mocking some girls, in the balls with one can and hits him with a second can in the head as he mumbles, "Sweet mother."

I guess it rang a bell.

Oh, the game. At half time it was Green Bay 21 Steelers 10. Not a bad half, if I could have spent some more time watching it without all the impedimenta.

Then came the Black Eyed Peas at half time. That's entertainment not a salad. I don't like peas, least of all black eyed ones and you can put cauliflower and squash into the melody of veggies.

And that's all I've got to say about that.

Just in case you didn't know a thirty second advertising spot during this Super Bowl sold for $2.8 to $3 million.

I guess it took 45 Super Bowls for the advertisers to finally get a bang for their buck, you see most of the ads either previewed earlier or in a collection of ads in numerous outlets on the Internet, many reaching an audience of more than 12 million.

Then, the ads that appeared during the Super Bowl reached another 100 million.

So, have a Pepsi Max in the balls if that's what turns you on, especially when it delivers zero calories – I guess that's if you don't drink it.

The best of the best ads, and I reviewed them all, perhaps was more of a comical delivery involving the Fox Sports analysts portrayed as E-Trade baby will talk, and it appeared in the pre-game show. The babies do a good job for E Trade without hitting someone in the balls.

Oh, the game . . . it was an exciting one as promised, rather ballsy if I didn't have all these distractions . . . Green Bay won 31 – 25 over the Steelers.

And, that's all I've got to say about all of this impedimenta.

THERE IS NO SUBSTITUTE FOR A HAMBURGER

New York (Storch Report) October 24, 2011 -- You can have all the cows from the Midwest mooing from the tops of sky scrapers in New York to eat more chicken, turkey or fowl, but there is no substitute for a hamburger that moos.

Oh, the food chemists keep trying with veggie, and soy burgers, sausage hot dogs corn dogs and chicken dogs, but nothing tastes as good as the real thing especially when it comes to a hamburger.

Last night I once again tried a turkey burger; the patty itself looked pale and unhealthy. I tried to bring some familiar taste looks and smell to my turkey patty by adding cheese, onion and ketchup but even that didn't help in fooling me.

I went on line today to get some reviews on substitutes, and more often than not hamburger connoisseurs who tried them threw away the remaining patties in the box.

We are going through a period of social correctness in everything from food to words.

In New York they have forced restaurants to take salt off the table, chefs to list the ingredients and calorie content on their menus. First lady Michelle Obama launched a program for schools through-out the United States to serve healthy meals because our kids are getting too fat.

Yet recently, while campaigning for the Dems, who need all the help they can get during the mid-term elections, she had a hamburger – yes the real thing.

Her hubby Barack, on more than one occasion has taken foreign dignitaries to his favorite DC hamburger joint, a place where all the meat moos, and being the guy he is, also brings back several bags of hamburgers for the White House staff. I guess the White House chef doesn't know how to make a good hamburger.

Campaigning last week, Obama had a glazed doughnut; I don't think it or hamburgers' are on Michelle's healthy food plan for kids.

In addition to declaring that salt is bad for us; sugar is also on the suggested list to curtail. Our government is suggesting that soda pop be taken out of our schools and is seeking the cooperation of soda companies.

When the first sugar substitutes came on the market they were so good for us that the FDA removed them because their side effects were causing more serious illnesses than just getting fat.. We don't know much more about the new batch than the old batch of sugar substitutes – time will tell.

The impact on the food industry has been so great that it's hard to pick up any package today without seeing the word healthy on the label.

I happen to think the real thing is the best thing and that whatever you consume should be done in moderation.

What happened to common sense? Did only our parents have it?

Even water can be dangerous, especially if you don't keep your head above it.

We bottle water, sell it at a high price even if its quality is not as good as what comes out the New York City tap.

All of this social correctness is so correct it is often incorrect and frequently boarders on dangerous.

A hamburger isn't bad for anyone once in a while, even the president. In fact I eat more turkey than anything else, especially off the bird, but I don't disguise it with hamburger meat.

I wonder what's going to happen to the rest of those turkey burger patties in our freezer.

BIRDS SQUIRRELS AND ME

Manasota Key FL (Storch Report) October 6, 2010 -- I guess it all started some six years ago when two on the starboard side of my house as you look east toward the entrance. They are rather formidable trees, for they tower over a three-story house and are just seconds from the food chain in the Gulf of Mexico to the west that makes the red roof on my garage white.

For a while it was a charming addition to my beach front property on a barrier reef on Manasota key that is until one evening I ran over a fish, larger than I can catch. It stuck to the tire on my car and the next morning my garage smelled like the Fulton fish market in Manhattan.

It was then that I thought of climbing the Norfolk pine and asking for some rental arrangement.

But after looking at the height of the tree, I thought better of the thought.

Now, as I understand it Ospreys are descendants of Eagles.

On one occasion my next store neighbor, an avid fisherman, caught a small fish and was releasing it from his line to throw it back from whence it came, when according to him, my Osprey swooped down and snatched it out of his hand. The Osprey's talons scratched his hand, but he said he wasn't going to sue.

I don't know where these birds screw or when, but sometime around Mother's Day they throw their newborns out of the nest and let them fly. Oh, and the parents help – I think.

A metaphor comes to mind every time I see this scene, I wish we could throw our President out of the White House and see if he can fly in this world in which an Osprey seems to survive even under these times of foreclosures.

But I'm getting off the subject.

A few years after the Osprey's arrived the migration of Robins from the East was absolutely extraordinary.

Somehow, they found my next door neighbor's property, whose hundreds of palm trees were not trimmed in decades and thousands of Robins became candidates for Betty Ford's clinic of alcoholism.

They eat the berries, get drunk, slam into windows and seek out water because they are dehydrated. We have a pool. The day they invaded, my house looked like a scene from Alfred Hitchcock's 'The Birds', I was running between the deck on the second floor of the house and the pool area chasing them away with a hose, only to realize that I was feeding their dehydration.

I really don't want to describe the mess. I had to call someone in to take care of it.

I think I'm as much of an environmentalist as Al Gore, I like flying in private jets, having multiple homes, spending bundles on electricity and winning the Nobel Prize, for environmental concerns.

So, I thought to myself – how about attracting small birds?

My wife's parents always liked Cardinals. I like them too – the male is prettier than the female.

How in the hell did that happen – was that the sign of the times to come? Sort of like don't ask don't tell?

Well, I decided that I was going to buy a bird feeder. Now, I don't go about things in a small way. So I researched-out the best bird feeder for small birds. I had enough big birds.

I came upon a National Geographic catalog, and there it was. A global bird feeder that would attract small birds, prevent squirrels from coming in and it was global in design, made of steel and only cost $50. That was my kind of bird feeder.

In fact the first thing that came to mind was that it was global in nature, you know we were no longer checking passports or birth certificates for presidents or who was crossing the border illegally, we were just redistributing wealth, so I thought, why not food.

It came by UPS and I couldn't wait to fill it up with bird seed. Hung it off the kitchen by my wife's desk and waited for the small birds and Cardinals.

And low and behold, a Cardinal came by grasped the bars of the globe, entered, had a snack, looked around and probably said to himself. 'What am I the bird man of Alcatraz?'

He never came back. I relocated the globe of a bird feeder to the upper deck and attached it to a railing in front of my office.

One day a Yellow Bird came by settled in and went in for a feast. I had a camera, took pictures, he seemed to like the scene. He even tried to get into my office, by banging into my window, but I think he saw his reflection in the window and was in love with himself.

A few days later he went away and never came back. I again relocated the expensive feeder near the pool. No one ever bothered it, not even the squirrels. The feeder rusted away, the seed as hard as Carmel popcorn from the Jersey shore.

But I wasn't going to give up. I reduced my expenses and bought bird feeders for an average price of $10, hung them under the soffits of the house and we got doves and cardinals and of course squirrels who ate most of the food.

The squirrels were chewing up the soffits with their paws to get to the bird feeders. I pulled down all the bird feeders. Repaired the soffits and repainted.

Put up a cedar pole, with a brass hanging holder and another expensive bird feeder in a sea of sea grapes. They, the squirrels had a field day. I thought I was dealing with just one squirrel, only to find out he had three other friends, who he must have told about the feast in my yard. They all came like it was a field of dreams climbing up the cedar pole as though I just designed it for them. Each patiently waited until one was full and then the next took its turn until the bird feeder food was finished off by the squirrels.

I took down the bird feeder and replaced it with a flower pot.

The next day one squirrel looked like he was impersonating the Statue of Liberty sitting on top of the pole with the flower pot below.

I went to Wall Mart and bought a $10 bird feeder called the Squirrel Stumper, it was a cage similar to the globe with the feed in the interior.

It was billed as a squirrel resistant metal cage, twist lock top with 8 feeding ports holding 3 lbs of seed.

Moved it back under the soffit.

Within no time the squirrel jumped from a ledge grabbed a hold of the cage and was munching away.

That afternoon I was talking to a colleague and he briefly excused himself because his young son came into his office and shot a dart gun at him.

He told me what had happened and I laughed, telling him the story of my problem with squirrels.

I said I was considering buying a water pistol to discourage the squirrels.

He said if I was going to do that he would suggest that I buy the 'Super Soaker', it was the best he said. He didn't recommend any knock off brands, because they broke down quickly.

So, I dashed out quickly to Wall Mart and bought two 'Super Soaker's' one for my wife and the other for myself. I figured we could break up the day in two shifts shooting this water soaker at squirrels so we could see cardinals.

Now this water whatever can be handled by anyone over the age of 6, so I thought my wife wouldn't have a problem. It has a distance up to 25 feet and its capacity of water ammo can be upgraded with ordinary large capacity soda bottles.

When I got home and before I could present my $7 present to my wife, and load my super soaker, the squirrel was feeding off of the squirrel stomper which I also bought at Wall Mart.

I don't know, but somehow the way things are going, I think this story is still developing . . .

BIG BUSINESS BOOM FOR BOOBS & BRAS-VERY UPLIFTING IN DOWN ECONOMY

Manasota Key FL (Storch Report) September 2, 2010 -- If you are a boob man you had a bonanza today if you read the New York Times, they had two features in one issue on boobs and bras.

When I first started reading the Gray Lady, those words were verboten.

My how times have changed, but it is encouraging to read some positive news when most businesses are down and the bra business is up with or without under wire support or a bra bailout.

However, I thought the stories were somewhat in conflict with each other.

The story out of New York says that most women wear the wrong size bra. And that's where Linda the Bra Lady comes in.

She, Linda Becker, says the wrong size bra is very uncomfortable and says it's like wearing the wrong size shoes. I guess I never thought of it that way, although I have had tight shoes, but never a tight bra.

I didn't know until I read these stories that the industry changed the sizes of bras six years ago.

Linda told the Times that her current bra size was a 34F. She said six years ago she was a 36D. In the interim she put on 40 pounds, noting that she put on a lot of weight in her breasts.

She also said she was 60, but humbly said she looks 40.

Today as the article reported the most popular size is an H cup and the largest size sold is a 54N.

I don't exactly know how to envision this.

She says she sells 4,000 bras a week with the most expensive bra being $129 and the least expensive $29.

She does all of this in 370 square feet and is running out of space, for she has bras from floor to ceiling. Business is so good she hands out those round discs that restaurants give to customers that buzz when it's your turn for a personal fitting to get the right size.

Apparently there is a lot of feeling going on in the fitting process of the bra business, because she says throughout a female's life breasts are changing.

I'm surprised there aren't more men in this field.

Linda says, "Some people gain a lot of weight in their breasts, which I do. All through life your breasts change. You work out, you have babies, you have a condition, you lose weight, you gain weight, you're lifting weights, and your back gets bigger. Sometimes you do none of these things and your breasts change."

She went on to say in the Times piece, "I always say breasts have a mind of their own. They're like two bad kids. If you don't control them, they're out of control."

I just never thought of them in that light.

A new approach for men might be, 'are the kid's behaving?'

Now the juxtaposition on this piece appeared on the Style page and it was featuring another niche on the West Coast where Ellen Shing, the owner of Lula Lu a boutique in San Mateo, Calif., caters to small boobs AAA-to A cup sizes. She says some come in her shop looking for padded bras, but says the majority "don't want to supersize themselves."

Shing says she isn't sure if the small-and loving-it attitude she has noticed is "about pride or more like being O.K. with who they are." But she says its fueling sales.

However, it was noted in this article that it was not uncommon for women with modest boobs to flaunt what little they've got with a deep V-neck cut or halter top.

It was noted that in the past the ironing board flat chested women were often told that they couldn't be helped or they were referred to the children's department for training bras.

I guess there's some good news for little boobs. On the positive side women do not experience pain from running or dancing, they can sleep on their stomachs and best of all sagging is minimal. And today they can go to Lula Lu and get a bra to enhance their cleavage allowing them to wear clothes that are sexier.

Neither of these stories appeared on the business page of the Times, nevertheless the niche in the booming bosom business whether uplifting or flat is a boon to these boutiques in a flat economic environment.

IT'S TIME FOR THE OUIJA BOARD

Washington DC (Storch Report) August 25, 2010 -- When all else fails, and we as a nation are now at that critical point of no return, it's time for President Obama to pull out all the stops, and I would suggest he bring out the Ouija Board.

Perhaps he should extend his present rainy 6th vacation of the year in Martha's Vineyard and spend some time to play this ancient board game with the first family.

After all, it might prove to be more productive than a soggy foggy beach, reading or playing basketball with the guys at an indoor gym. It also could be fun for the first family including Bo, the first dog, with paws- in which might provide more answers to the nation's job picture, real estate doldrums and economic woes, than all the Czars attached to his Cabinet.

I don't know about you and your connection to this board game, but my parents bought a Ouija Board and we often played the game, rather than listen to The Shadow or FBI on the radio.

I was always amazed at how that heart-shaped piece of wood would move over the board. You had to touch it lightly, but I could never determine whether my partner was moving the piece of wood, rather than me. In retrospect, perhaps it was a lot like politics, in its movements.

Ouija is a talking board which spells out messages. The board is marked with letters, numbers and other symbols to communicate with spirits. The pancetta – the small heart-shaped piece of wood – spells out the message during a séance.

Can you ever think of a better time for a séance than now?

The board was introduced in the late 1890's and was considered to be a harmless parlor game.

That is until mainstream Christian – something Obama claims to be – religions and some occultists associated its use with the threat of demonic possession and some have cautioned followers not to use Ouija boards.

While Ouija believers feel the paranormal or supernatural is responsible for Ouija's action, I would rather believe that it is more parsimoniously explained by unconscious movements of those controlling the pointer, a psychological phenomenon known as the ide motor effect.

Whatever, Mr. President play the game? Let Bo have paws-on – we couldn't do any worse!

MCDONALD'S STATIN ISLAND BURGER OR NATHAN'S VIAGRA DOG?

New York (Storch Report) August 14, 2010 -- Barack forces taxpayers to own Government Motors, Banks, have health insurance whether they want it or not, Michele forces our kids to eat healthy, and now a cardiologist from the UK wants MacDonald's to handout statin pills with each Big Mac they serve.

Next, someone will be forcing Nathan's to serve up Viagra with each hot dog.

We have become a nation of government run nincompoops with no rights or ability to make our own decisions under a Constitution that only works the way Obama wants it to work, like building a Mosque next to Ground Zero and not enforcing immigration laws and Allah forbid if a State wants to uphold the law, Obama will sue them.

If all of this wasn't so serious it would be funny.

Can you imagine going out for a hot dog and your wife looks at you and says, "Honey not now, the kids are in the back seat. You should have had a hamburger at least that would have raised your HDL's."

Life is getting so intrusive these days, a neighbor left his computer on overnight and Microsoft downloaded an update. When he got up in the morning he was notified of the download and the restarting of his computer. There was a message that said he could click on the icon and find out what was downloaded. He did, and the message was encrypted.

A few days later Obama's Health Patrol, a spinoff of the Death Panel, called and requested my neighbor go to the doctor.

The doctor had a full report from the Health Patrol on my neighbor's sleep patterns and excessive snoring. They diagnosed sleep apnea. He now wears a mask at night and shuts down his computer.

It is so confusing today that what is left is right and what is right is wrong.

The suggestion from the cardiologist about a burger and a statin was actually based upon a study. You see statins are cholesterol-lowering drugs and they do prevent heart attacks and strokes and this study calculated that the reduction in heart disease risk offered by a statin could offset the increase in risk from eating a cheeseburger and a milkshake. Statins do lower the bad cholesterol and raise the good cholesterol.

Statins have something in common with Viagra, both raise and lower something.

You see when people engage in risky behaviors like driving or smoking they're encouraged – no that's the wrong word today is forced – to take measures that minimize their risk like wearing a seat belt or stopping smoking, or not talking on the cell phone when driving.

We also have something in common with the Brits, because there is socialized medicine on both sides of the pond now.

When I was a kid I had a dog, a black and white cocker spaniel named Pudgy and even he had more rights then, than I have now. When the Vet recommended we give him some pills to prevent worms he suggested that we put the pill inside some hamburger meat and that he would swallow the pill while eating the meat.

Pudgy ate the meat and spit out the pill.

A PRELUDE TO MICHELLE'S VACATION

Washington DC (Storch Report) August 8, 2010 -- Before Michelle Obama went on her extravagant vacation with Sasha, a bevy of friends, staff and Secret Service Agents to Spain this week she must have had a discussion about it with President Obama before she left. I'll bet it went something like this:

M: "Barack, I'm thinking about taking Sasha to Spain this summer for a vacation. Being that Malia is in camp it gives me a chance to bond with my youngest."

B: "When are you planning to do this?"

M: "I was thinking of the week of August 2nd."

B: "For how long?"

M: I thought we would go for about 8 days."

B: "That's the week of my 49th birthday."

M: "Oh, you can bond with first dog Bo, and then go for a private night of dining with Oprah Winfrey, Gayle King and some friends in Chicago"

B: "You get to go to Spain at some posh resorts and sightseeing and I get a night in Chicago on my birthday? You know, that's not quite what I had in mind when I spoke of 'wealth redistribution'. How are you getting there?

M: "I'm planning to take Air Force 2."

B: "Michelle do you know that plane is a 757 and costs the taxpayer $11,000 an hour to fly."

M: "We'll reimburse them for a round-trip first class ticket."

B: "The difference Michelle between a first class ticket and the use of that plane, is $176,000 of taxpayer money."

M: "Well, I worked hard to get to this place and I'm sure as hell going to take advantage of it. How many other black women have had this opportunity?"

B: "You have a point there, what else are you planning to do on this trip?"

M: "My staff has worked out an agenda. We are planning to stay at the Hotel Villa Padierna in the mountains outside Marbella. It has two golf courses, a posh spa with Turkish baths, views of the Mediterranean Sea and a superb restaurant."

B: "How much a room?"

M: "Room rates start at $400 and elevate to $6,500 for a two-bedroom villa with a private pool and 24-hour butler service, we will probably take the latter. There is also planned a Hollywood star-studded gala the last night we are at the hotel. We also expect the Spaniards to shut down one of their public beaches for a day so Sasha and I can take a swim. We are planning to visit with King Juan Carlos and Queen Sofia on Sunday at their summer residence on the island of Mallorca. We can legitimately write this off to the taxpayer."

B: "How much do you think the entire trip will cost?"

M: "Between $300,000 and $500,000."

B: "Jesus Christ, Michelle how am I going to explain all of this to the public? The numbers, the amount we pay and what the taxpayer pays?

M: "Jesus Christ? I think you got your religions mixed up. As for the explanation you're good at that with your silver tongue. Get the teleprompter out."

B: Michelle, this is just bad timing . . . I can't believe you are going to do this, especially with the economy having high unemployment, we have a jittery stock market, I have preached sacrifice and fiscal discipline to the people and things are looking bad for the mid-term elections. How, am I going to deal with this?"

M: "Very frankly my dear, I don't give a damn."

FLIGHT 775

Miami FL (Storch Report) July 14, 2010 -- Travel is so much fun these days I haven't been doing much of it. But recently I reacquainted myself with what I have been missing.

It all began with the emptying of the bags I just packed and undressing what I just put on to the point that my pants were falling down because I had no belt, and then I found myself shoeless, somewhat like Joe Jackson before I stepped into a full body scan.

Once scanned I was immediately asked what I had in my left hand shirt pocket? I said I have my boarding ticket and my passport which you require. "Take both out of your pocket and hold it in your left hand," the TSA agent said.

Then he said," What do you have in your right hand pants pocket?" I said, "Money". He said, "Show me." And I pulled out a wad of cash. He said, "Okay."

So I asked him if he found anything else. He said what do you mean? I said, well as a taxpayer I just paid for a full body scan. How was everything hanging, did you find any cancer or heart disease? After all there must be some benefit to me for paying for this full body scan where you examined every part of my anatomy? Or, is this just a possible health hazard that my next of kin will find out about long after I am gone?

He said, "You know sir what we are looking for." I said, "Yes, and you found it – my cash! However, I wish you would send a report on the scan to my doctor."

I then proceeded to re-pack and re-dress. I was in the brand spanking new American Airlines terminal at Miami Airport and running late due to an accident on one of the off ramps and as you might suspect my departure gate was D44. Yes, it seemed as though it was 44 miles from my full body scan.

I was one of the last to board. My very attentive Flight Attendant asked me if I would like a drink, I said, "Yes, I could use one after going through a complete medical exam going through screening and walking 44 miles to catch this flight. I'll have a gin and tonic."

I was on my way to St. Thomas with a final destination of St. John.

We were about an hour into the flight and I was into my second gin and tonic and my very attentive Flight Attendant asked me if I would be joining 'us' for lunch. I said sure, but I didn't know if it was with him or the first class section.

I asked him if we were on a 777, because the plane was configured in a very similar way. "Oh, thank you, but no, this is a 757 with a new interior design."

"I know you gave me some headsets for music, but I'm not getting any sound. And, is there a movie? He said, "I'm sorry but our audio and video system is frozen and I can't un-stick it."

I said, "Yes I see that, the man in the instructional video is still putting on his life vest for a water landing."

"We have for lunch today Tortellini or Steak."

"I'll have the steak," I said.

About a half hour later he was back with his clip board and pencil and said we have a change in the menu. I said, "In midflight?"

He said, "Yes the steak is actually chicken."

I said, "Did we fly into a flock?"

"No it was a computer mix-up."

"I'll have the chicken, as long as it's not clucking."

IT'S ALL BUSH'S FAULT

Washington DC (Storch Report) June 27, 2010 -- Barack: "Michelle, look what I inherited now. Look at these damn embarrassing photos!"

Barack: "Honey, it's not funny."

Michelle: "Oh Barack, stop taking yourself so seriously."

Barack: Seriously? This place is infested with bees, flies and rats."

Michelle: "Well honey, you knew about the latter . . . you brought them with you."

Barack: "You know, I'm not in the mood for a play on words."

Michelle: "Well, I just think you have to lighten-up a bit."

Barack: "Look at this one . . . me with a fly on my lip. It's enough to make one stutter while reading the teleprompter. And this one in the Rose garden with a rat running in front of my podium. This is the White House, not some ACORN office in Chicago. Soon, I won't be able to hold a press conference in the Rose Garden for all the damn bees."

Michelle: "Barack, you certainly aren't going to blame George W. Bush for this one?"

Barack: "Why not, if he can take the blame for the breakup of Al and Tipper Gore, he can take the blame for the infestation of all of these varmints. He probably brought them up here from Texas."

DO WE HAVE A CHOICE?

Washington DC (Storch Report) June 18, 2010 -- O: "I don't think so."

BP: "But we brought oil to your shores."

O: "You sure have."

BP: "Your country is addicted to oil."

O: "We sure are, but you will pay for your recklessness."

BP: "This sounds like Chicago-style politics?"

O: "Call it what you will."

BP "You finally invite us to the White house, but all you want is our open ended check book."

O: "You got it!"

BP: "I thought this was a Democracy?"

O: "Sometimes it is."

BP: "You want us to give you an open ended check, initially for $20 Billion plus another $100 Million, while you have opened an investigation threatening our executives with criminal charges?"

O: "Yes."

BP: "Sounds like a shake-down to us with no quid pro quo?"

O: "Call it what you will – my political career is on the line."

BP: "With the substantial amount of money that's on the table there must be some room for horse trading."

O: "I didn't say there wasn't. But I must maintain my public persona of toughness – you know, like in 'kicking ass.' Deliver what

I ask and I will see the JD doesn't bring charges. Provide me with evidence that this oil spill was an accident."

BP: "You should be thanking us – this crisis plays into your energy plan of cap and tax. We understand 'you never allow a serious crisis go to waste?"

O: "That's what I hear too. But I also never let the facts get in the way of a good crisis. Your CEO is testifying tomorrow before Congress. He must keep his cool, because he will be sliced and diced. Admit nothing, just have him speak to the people and tell them BP is prepared to do what is right, stop the spill, mitigate the damage and compensate those that have suffered a loss."

BP: "Why don't you accept clean-up help from the Dutch, they have the expertise in these types of spills?"

O: "That is an internal matter that will help my personal political agenda."

BP: "In other words it helps to escalate the crisis and leads you to your energy agenda?"

O: "Yes, and in addition by not waving the Jones Act I am again delivered the Union vote in 2012."

BP: "Sure sounds like a complex shakedown to us?"

O: "Call it what you will, but you get to stay in business, recoup your investment when gas reaches $7 a gallon and it's a win win for all."

INFIDELITY IS ALL IN THE RING FINGER

New York (Storch Report) April 26, 2010 -- I went for a drink at Elaine's with my friend Dino in Manhattan and sat alongside a rather attractive middle aged woman with breasts that seemed to be seeking relief.

We ordered two Tanqueray's on the rocks with a twist.

Dino, a New York City detective, saw the scene and said, "Cool it, you don't know who she's with, or who she might be waiting for."

"Well", I said, "the guy alongside of her is with his date, she seems to be alone."

"Yeh, but she may be waiting for someone."

"Well, we'll wait and see."

"I don't know if you noticed," Dino, "she doesn't have a ring on her ring finger and that finger is longer than the second finger."

"What does that mean?"

"Well, did you see Dr. Phil on 'The View' today? He says people with ring fingers – you know that's the fourth one – that is longer than the second one are more likely to be untrue to their husbands or significant others."

"You've got to be kidding. You mean infidelity? You're not listing to that crap?"

"No," Dino, "this has been proven scientifically."

"Look", Dino, "her drink is almost empty, I'm going to buy her one."

I turned to her and asked if I might buy her a drink.

"What are you having?"

She answered, "An apple martini."

I nodded to the bartender and told him to give her a refill and to put it on my bill.

"What's your name?" I asked.

She said "Buffy."

"Buffy", I said, "Are you from the Hampton's?"

She said no, she was from Brooklyn.

"Brooklyn, wow I had a tryout with the Brooklyn Dodgers at Ebbets Field."

"How did it work out?"

"Not too well with them, but had a lot of fun playing ball."

Making a rather smooth segue I said, "Do you know your ring finger, which doesn't have a ring, is longer than your second finger?"

"Well, I haven't really noticed, but so what?"

"Do you watch 'The View' . . . well they had Dr. Phil on today and he says that studies show that a person with a ring finger that is longer than the second finger is more likely to have infidelity tendencies? You're ring finger is longer than the second finger . . . so is mine. Did you ever have you're L33 gene checked?"

"My L33 gene?"

"Yes, that's the one that shows that if you have two copies of this allele you would have twice the risk of experiencing marital dysfunction, with the threat of divorce."

With that she picked up her bag, thanked me for the drink and walked out of Elaine's.

Dino said, "That worked well!"

"Yeh, I kind of burned and crashed."

"But she did say goodbye when she got to the door," Dino said.

"What did she say?"

"She gave you the finger."

"Which one?"

"The third one."

OBAMA LAME STREAM MEDIA OUTAGE WHILE CROSSING THE ATLANTIC

On-board the Regent Seven Seas Mariner (Storch Report) March 27, 2010 -- — Somewhere two days into a 6-day crossing of the Atlantic from the island of Bermuda to the island of Madeira off of Portugal, my daily 'Passages' the shipboard news of the day, informed me of the following:

"Due to moving out of the satellite signal area, please be advised that we will lose reception of CNN, TNT and ESPN until we reach Funchal, Wednesday, March 31st. This is a normal occurrence when crossing the Atlantic (and Pacific). We will have FOX News as it comes to us through our Internet connection. We apologize for any inconvenience caused."

'Inconvenienced caused?' I mean after all, didn't this cruise line realize that the Obama administration declared FOX News a non-news station? Are they trying to tell me that CNN couldn't make the same Internet arrangements?

It sounds to me much like a right wing, tea party conspiracy — so far I haven't seen any threatening pirates, but I'm on the look-out.

Fortunately, I was able to catch VP Joe Biden on CNN on the first leg of the trip from Ft. Lauderdale to Bermuda calling the signing of Obamacare a 'F***g big deal' from President Obama's office of dignity.**

I knew that Obamacare reached this cruise line when I dined in the Compass Rose, the main dining room of the ship.

Health care reform recommended that all of the chairs in the dining room be replaced with seats for the svelte.

I guess this is part of the preventive Obamacare program in contrast to the death panel.

A normal sized man or women with an acceptable body mass index (BMI) has difficulty fitting into these chairs, especially if wearing a suit or jacket. You fit if you put the jacket outside of the arms of the chair.

Oh, and the arms of the chair, they are so short the Doctor's office had a run on chin lacerations from people leaning on the arms and slipping off.

Many were seen leaving the dining room with the chairs stuck to their BMI.

Now we haven't addressed the modestly overweight, considering the average on-board age being in the 70 s, a cruising age that doesn't exactly represent the svelte.

For these individuals there were chairs held in reserve – without arms.

Embarrassing, yes for those that didn't fit and those that fit. The chairs were exchanged for all to see who needed to visit the fitness center.

Fortunately, thanks to a cost cutting move, the paparazzi was not on board.

Obamacare has a fall-out beyond belief.

As far as the lame stream media, I guess I'll have to deal with the fair and balanced reporting of the non-news station, FOX News until I get to Funchal.

MR. PRESIDENT, LET'S DO WHAT YOU DO BEST – PERFORM!

Washington DC (Storch Report) February 8, 2010 -- Over the weekend while a blizzard rolled into Washington DC, ignoring all signs of the administration's projections of climate warming, President Obama called a meeting in the oval office of his key advisers, Rahm Emanuel and David Axelrod to discuss the next steps in health care reform, which he openly refuses to accept is dead in the water.

The meeting took place before the president held an interview with CBS's Katie Couric prior to the Super Bowl. It was a classic Saul Alinsky community organizing strategy meeting. And, Emanuel and Axelrod, both Alinsky believers, called it for what it was before the meeting.

Obama: "Rahm, David you know I'm not going to give up on health care reform and as you know I have an interview prior to the Super Bowl with Couric and we know the subject of health care will come up, among many others. Your thoughts?"

Emanuel: "Mr. President, I think we have a chance to turn this around even if we don't get a bill for now. I think we should invite both Democratic and Republican leaders to an open televised meeting to clear the air and to solicit ideas on health care from both parties."

Obama: "Yes, but I don't want to give up any ground on either the house or senate bills."

Emanuel: "With all due respect Mr. President, you excel in your performance and this is an opportunity to perform. Perhaps not to the point you are going to convince those up for election this year, but perhaps you can, during the public meeting, show that the Republicans are obstructionists – that will be a political gain for any Democrat running in 2010. We know they will come up with the usual, crossing state lines for insurance, tort reform and proposing that we start over with bipartisan discussions."

Obama: "I'm not starting over."

Axelrod: "Mr. President, I think Rahm has an idea, although it may be a strategy that keeps us in a holding pattern for now. Allow me to remind you of a chapter in Saul Alinsky's book "Rules for Radicals", I think it was the chapter on communication. I looked it up; allow me to quote an excerpt:

"Much of the time . . . the organizer will have a pretty good idea of what the community should be doing, and he will want to suggest, maneuver, and persuade the community toward that action. He will not ever seem to tell the community what to do; instead, he will use loaded questions.

"And so the guided questioning goes on without anyone losing face or being left out of the decision-making. Every weakness of every proposed tactic is probed by questions.

"Eventually someone suggests a tactic and again through questions, its positive features emerge and it is decide on."

Alinski goes on, Axelrod notes: "Is this manipulation? Certainly, just as a teacher manipulates, and no less even a Socrates. As time goes on and education proceeds, the leadership becomes increasingly sophisticated. The organizer recedes from the local circle of decision makers . . . his job becomes one of weaning the group away from any dependency upon him. Then his job is done."

"Mr. President, this is the way we should go. It shows transparency and through a subliminal approach we cast the blame on the other party."

Obama: "I think this is good, I will tell Couric that we will call a Summit later this month and go through systematically all the best

ideas that are out there and move it forward. I will tell her that I want to look at the Republican ideas that are out there. And I want to be very specific. For example, how do you guys want to lower costs? How do you guys intend to reform the insurance markets so people with preexisting conditions, for example, can get health care? I'll tell her that if we can go step by step through a series of these issues and arrive at some agreements, than procedurally, there's no reason why we can't do it a lot faster than the process took last year."

Emanuel: "That's it Mr. President, you lead by asking questions and raising issues about cost. This will begin to shift the attention to the GOP and portray them as obstructionists. My other suggestion is to not hold this at the White House. Let's pick a neutral ground, like the Blair House. It doesn't cast the imprimatur of the heavy handiness of the White House. Mr. President, you are a performer – you can pull this off."

Obama: "It's like Kabuki theatre."

Emanuel: "You got it, Mr. President."

THE GAME WAS BETTER THAN THE ADS

Manasota Key FL (Report) February 8, 2010 -- China opted out of taking an ad during the Super Bowl . . . Carrie Underwood should strike the National Anthem from her repertoire . . . The Who was upstaged by the glitz of light works – they would have done better singing 'Who's dat saying who's dat with their pants on the ground' . . . and it seemed that the economy – with a $400,000 discount per 30 second ad – lacked commercial creativity and the game won out over the ads.

The sentimental favorites, the New Orleans Saints won the Super Bowl, over the 5-point favorites – the Indianapolis Colts 31-17.

I'm glad I'm not a betting man for I would have thought China, with all the money we owe them, might have returned some of it by taking out an ad during the Super Bowl for a 30 second travel commercial to the Great Wall. It would have only cost those $2.6 million, a $400,000 discount over last year's cost.

Then again everyone thought Payton Manning had the edge over Drew Brees, but they didn't understand the spirit of the French Quarter.

I was there years ago when Pete Fountain and Al Hirt played in their own clubs on Bourbon Street and Archie Manning was the quarterback for the perennial loosing Saints

People don't understand what bourbon does to a street.

In the next few days Mardi gras will come to New Orleans two weeks early.

And if you were a Super Bowl watcher to see the ads rather than the game, you really must have been disappointed.

The ads were as disappointing as the entertainment. I don't want to single out all the bad ads, for there were too many.

However, there was one Doritos' ad that stood out over the few bad one's they ran.

It was that kid who was protecting his single Mom – and his Doritos'. Guy walks into the house, eyes his date, sits on couch while waiting for his date to get ready and grabs a Dorito from a bowl on the cocktail table and the kid slaps the Dude in the face and says, "Keep your hands off my Mama and keep your hands off my Doritos'"

This was in contrast to a house full of beer cans advertising Bud Light – which fell flat.

It was much better years ago when Budweiser had their Clydesdale's kick a field goal.

Oh, the kid ads of the past for E-Trade also seem to be better yesterday than today, you know, the one where the kid calls a golfing partner 'shankapotomus'.

They can't use that kid anymore, he is four-years-old now.

There seems to be a correlation between the economy and advertising's creativity. I don't know if anyone in the beltway has given any thought to this?

However, the game was good and I'm happy for New Orleans.

OBAMA'S BOOKENDS

Washington DC (Storch Report) February 2, 2010 -- I don't know about you, but I have often wondered what it must feel like to be President Obama's bookend while he is delivering a major policy announcement on a subject of a Cabinet member's expertise and responsibility?

The heads of high power positions in the United States such as the Vice President, Secretaries of State, Defense, Treasury, Commerce, Health, etc, etc, etc stand by the president at parade rest as props while he makes a policy statement dealing with subjects of their responsibility and appear as speechless Mimes.

The bookends don't often smile – for there is not much to smile about these days.

They don't laugh in this scene for there is nothing to laugh about.

And they don't talk, because no one can talk as well as Obama.

When they go home from work and their kids ask them what they did today, they say without a smile, "I was a bookend."

It's not easy to be a bookend, it takes a lot of practice.

I remember when I was in the United States Navy we practiced putting one foot in front of another when we marched. It wasn't easy for some.

We practiced standing at attention and parade rest.

Bookends stand at parade rest.

They must have seminars for bookends in Washington DC.

It probably lasts three days and some outside consultant makes millions conducting these sessions.

The goal:

- **To support the subject matter as an icon from that office.**
- **Learning how to keep a stern face.**
- **Learning how to clasp your hands in front of you.**
- **Spreading your legs in a comfortable position, for you never know how long the speech will be.**
- **To standby the president – for he is lonely**
- **And, to take the blame if what the president says doesn't work.**

I wonder if the bookends know how silly they look, or, perhaps they feel proud when asked by the president to be a bookend.

For after all, they are a symbol of support, kind of like wires holding up a newly planted tree.

I wonder if there is a White House Czar of bookends.

THE PRESIDENT'S NEW SUIT

Washington DC (Storch Report) January 26, 2010 -- Once upon a time there lived an arrogant, vain, articulate good looking President whose only worry in life was to redistribute wealth, much like in the image of Robin Hood. He thought government could cure all, take care of everyone and the more he appeared before his people the more they would admire him and he could bamboozle them with his agenda.

He mastered the teleprompter like none other, but there were times when the teleprompter faltered or crashed to the floor and he was not as articulate as he appeared to be without it. He was in the people's face as often as possible to disseminate his progressive thesis.

He was smooth, and with a playbook out of the left suggesting socialism with supporters within his administration boasting the likes of Communistic leanings and admiring the likes of Mao, Che, Chavez and Fidel, but the people didn't seem to recognize what was going on because this cool dude, appearing with the lanky and toned arms of his wife at his side, continued to spin the same yarn that put him in office.

His campaign promises were quickly forgotten by the people and him and he was being given a free ride by the media – it was more than a honeymoon.

He traveled the world apologizing for the Nation's past and was welcomed wherever he went putting down his country with his hidden agenda.

It was all of what he inherited and he was about to change all of this by putting as much as he could on his plate in his first year in office, because the more rapidly he could push through his agenda the better the nation would be. He wanted health care reform – everyone should be covered including illegal aliens.

He wanted climate change. He wanted to stimulate the economy because it was in bad shape – so he stimulated it by spending, jobs were lost at a rapid rate, people lost their houses, banks failed, he bailed out Wall Street, the auto industry and the banking industry. Unemployment soared, but he stayed the course with health care for a full year.

He met with his advisers and them all told him his old suit was working. It was still a full house. The people were buying it, despite some naysayers. They suggested quelling the right wing media with the 'fairness doctrine'.

"Damn the torpedoes, full steam ahead."

He was weak on defense, gave terrorists a free ride when caught and wanted to free those that were captured because of his left wing leanings.

Meanwhile the President's party lost gubernatorial elections in Virginia and New Jersey, trips to Europe failed to bring home the Olympics to Chicago and a trip to Copenhagen to sell climate warming resulted in a cold freeze. His polls dipped to new lows.

The President was likable, affable but didn't seem to have any coattails.

Now the President was ready to ram the health care bill through, with full control of his party when out of nowhere a tea party erupted in Boston and a Republican Senatorial candidate upset a Democratic candidate in a stronghold held for decades by the Democrats.

The voters in Massachusetts, said, "The President is naked."

The next day in the Oval office the President's advisers said, "Mr. President you need to change suit."

I thank the tailor from Copenhagen, Hans Christian Anderson for allowing me to update a good story.

IT'S SO COLD IN FLORIDA, NO ONE'S TALKING ABOUT THE EARLY BIRD SPECIAL

Manasota Key FL (Storch Report) January 10, 2010 -- I was so comforted this morning after I reintroduced myself to my golf clubs in the garage after more than two weeks of no golf to find out from the New York Times that this cold thing that I'm feeling here has to do with 'Arctic oscillation' and that I can now re-direct my attention to the early bird special here on the west coast of south Florida.

I'm really not interested in food, and I hate early bird specials. But that's not typical here, especially with the snow birds.

But the Times enlightened me. They assured me that what's going on has nothing to do with Global cooling?

Al Gore must have gotten to them.

You see, as they tell it, it is has to do with, "Arctic oscillation, in which opposing atmospheric pressure patterns at the top of the planet occasionally shift back and forth, affecting weather across much of the Northern Hemisphere."

Well that's fine, but I didn't move to Florida to be cold. And I'm tired of Al Gore telling me how warm it's getting and winning prizes for it.

If I wanted to be cold I would move to North Dakota, and I really don't want to hear from them about how cold it is – that's where they selected to be.

If I select to go to the early bird special in Florida, I don't expect to wear something I don't have – ear muffs.

They say in the Times that what is most notable this year is that the pattern of high pressure over the Arctic is more pronounced than at any time since 1950. Well for God sakes, I wasn't even out of high school then.

They go on to say, "In most years over the past few decades, the opposite has been true there has been lower than average pressure over the Arctic, and higher than average pressure over the mid-latitudes — the middle of which cuts through Maine, across the Great Lakes and on to Oregon."

The best line in this piece that seems to defend global warming while I am re-introducing myself to my golf clubs in the garage, "No one is quite sure what drives these flip-flops in air pressure."

I thought flip flops were what I used to wear in Florida.

There are really some crazy things going on today, I mean the economy isn't very good, jobs have gone somewhere else, houses are not worth what it takes to pay off the mortgage, Bill Clinton thinks the President would be fetching coffee a few years ago and Harry Reid says our President speaks well for a Negro.

I don't know Al, all I want to be is warm in Florida.

PROFILING

Manasota Key FL (Storch Report) January 9, 2010 -- I've been doing something just about all of my life which might be considered politically incorrect – profiling.

I never thought much about it before 9/11, but upon reflection when I am at a cocktail party and a woman walks into the room and has an outstanding figure the first thing that comes to mind is that country and western song, "If I told you, you had a beautiful body would you hold it against me?"

I suppose one might call this lecherous, but when God gives you something to admire call it what you will and I will be the admirer.

I'll bet my profiling addiction went all the way back to my childhood. I think that's the way I picked my friends.

I never hung around kids that were constantly in trouble. Perhaps that was my parents influence.

Parents, of which I am one, are known to deliver certain prejudices to their off-spring and profiling is probably one of them.

My profiling became much more sophisticated as I got older. If I found someone to be a bore, I avoided them.

Now if they were female with a voluptuous body, I turned down my hearing aid.

It wasn't until color came into pictures that profiling became more complex, before that everything was black or white.

Now we have shades of everything today, to the point we can't tell friend from foe.

Oh, there are some giveaways, like beards, skin-heads, tattoo's, rings in the nose, tongue, ears, belly button and some unmentionable places.

I became astutely aware of my profiling addiction during my freshman year in college when my English professor required all of his students to make five observations of people a day, record them on three by five cards, and be prepared, at a moment's notice, to report on their observations.

I loved this part of the class and it sure did help me later on when I became a journalist.

I don't know about you, but when I create a profile of someone they are put into buckets.

I have buckets for voluptuous women, bores, shady characters, ugly and obnoxious people, left wingers, right wingers, conservatives, golfers that can't count, newly formed tea party activists, people that wear sheets, beards veils, burka's, Muslims and of course terrorists.

I firmly believe if the person is wearing a veil, a burka, beard, sheet, the name spells like alphabet soup and you can't pronounce it, it's a terrorist first and a Muslim second.

I don't know if they have a rehab place for a profiling addiction, but I never thought of going to one.

IF YOU CAN'T PRONOUNCE THE NAME – IT'S A TERRORIST!

Washington DC (Storch Report) January 5, 2010 -- I don't want to over simplify or be over critical of our security systems in the United States, but something struck me this evening after realizing how many TV anchors across our land flubbed the pronunciation of the Christmas Day suspects' name who tried to blow up the Northwest Airlines flight from Amsterdam to Detroit culminating with President Obama's declaration this evening of a US intelligence failure when the teleprompter pro couldn't pronounce Umar Farouk Abdulmutallab's name either. I thought to myself there's the answer to preventing terrorism – if you can't pronounce the name, profile the passenger as a terrorist.

Eureka, I thought, the answer to difficult or complex problems is in its simplicity.

I mean after all if it looks like the alphabet and you can't pronounce it – it requires further scrutiny.

I mean, after all our intelligence community is too bright to see dots and then logically connect them. This was a difficult case. The man's name, who I can't pronounce, was on a US list of suspects; he traveled from Nigeria, had been to Yemen – a hot bed of Al Qaeda – moved on to Amsterdam on a one way ticket for which he paid cash, banned from entering the UK, his father warned the

US Embassy that he was a Jihad leaning young man, told his father that this was the last time he would be speaking to him and was still allowed passage to Detroit with no luggage where his attempt to blow up the plane was foiled by a heroic crew and passengers.

There really weren't enough clues to suspect this passenger from wrong doing. The only thing Intel overlooked was his name because that nearly had every letter of the alphabet and to pull him aside for alphabet soup questioning really wouldn't be politically correct. I mean how are we going to deal with the Greeks, the Polish or for that matter the Russians or others from Slovak countries?

But if I were president I would think about sending a directive to TSA that if they can't pronounce the name they should consider the passenger a terrorist. Now I don't know how linguistic members of the TSA are, but what would be the harm, anyone with a name like that would understand the questioning.

I hope the president takes my suggestion seriously, for its simple and very economical as compared to the technology being considered and the future radiation Americans will be exposed to, exposing everything the tabloids are looking for, resulting in cancer and a further burden on our Health Care system.

I was also impressed with the President's rapid response to this crisis. Let's see it occurred on December 25 and the administration initially said our security system worked. Four days later while Obama was on vacation in Hawaii they suggested it didn't work too well and they dodged a bullet. But that didn't bring Obama home until he was ready to come home. Now 11 days later he calls the event a failure of US intelligence to piece it all together. Aside from Obama being on vacation, perhaps he's out to lunch.

Mr. President let's make it simple – if you Barack Hussein Obama can't pronounce the name, let's check them out as a terrorist.

THREE CLICKERS IN THE FAMILY ROOM

Irvington NJ (Storch Report) December 20, 2009 -- I can remember it as though it was yesterday. It was the early 50's and my family bought its first TV.

It was a 10 inch Emerson, rather an oblong design to handle the TV tube. Everyone could turn it on.

There was an on off button, much like a radio in those days and a dial that would change the channels.

When you turned it on and got a test pattern that was sharp and clear you would watch it.

There were Sunday's when the Ed Sullivan hour would come on and you were amazed when a black and white image appeared on the screen, with song dance and music. Beyond that there was wrestling. Some thought it was real in those days.

Seventy years later I have one of those flat TV digital screens, 42 inches, with those three challenging clickers and hundreds of channels, none with a test pattern. Beyond this TV we have four more and they have clickers, all of which require knowledge of the clickers to make them work.

I don't like it, but I'm the only one in the house that knows how to work the five TVs, all of which become more difficult when you have Blue Ray DVD players, obsolete VHS recorders and some TVs with a combo of all the modern devices including memory cards.

Have you ever tried to explain to a guest how to handle one TV with three clickers, not alone four more in guest rooms with multiple clickers? By the time you get finished with the instructions, it's time for the guests to leave.

And then you don't know what they have learned or remember for their return visit.

And none of this has anything to do with when we have a power failure or surge and the TV needs to be rebooted and in which order the clickers need to be re-sequenced

For the sake of a shorter story, let's stay with three clickers in the family room.

After some 20 years in this house my wife decides that it is time that she should know how to work the TV. So I begin my remedial TV instructions and she takes notes.

We begin with the Comcast TV clicker. You push the all on button – that's the red one – and sometimes that puts on both the TV and the cable box.

If you notice that the blue light is not on the Sharp Aqueous TV then you need to turn on the on button on the Sharp clicker.

Once you have a picture on the TV screen you will notice the TV Guide comes up on the screen. Well that doesn't work. You now have to pick up the Sharp clicker and push TV menu. That gets rid of the menu screen and you can go to the channel of your choice. You can do this by punching in the numbers or doing the channel search – you know that's when I click through a hundred channels that disturbs you so.

Now you are in the TV mode. I know that there are times you want to watch a flick.

Well in order to get in the flick mode. You must pick up the Sharp clicker, push input to get out of the HD TV mode and into input 2 which allows you to access the Sony Blue Ray DVD. Now you pick up the Sony clicker and push on.

You will see that the tray opens up on the DVD player. You insert the DVD and push play – oh, that's not the one labeled play, it's the one in the center of all those north, south, east, west, arrows and don't ask

me why, it's just the way it is — and you will see a bunch of previews, in order to not watch them all don't push the advance button, push the arrow buttons and that will move the previews forward. Again, don't ask me why this is the way it is – it's just the way it is!

Now to get back to where you once were in order to shut off the TV you just reverse the order of these instructions and then shut off the all off button – that's the red one – and everything should go off. If you notice that the TV still seems to be on then you pick up the Sharp clicker and turn off the TV.

Yes, my dear there were simpler days, and I do miss watching the Test Pattern.

THE 21ST CENTURY CHARADE

Manasota Key FL (Storch Report) December 18, 2009 -- We are nearly 10 years into the 21st Century and we didn't get off to a very good start with the likes of 9/11.

But the Bush administration kept us safe from further threats on our soil for the next 8 years since that catastrophic radical Muslim attack on our nation, which many seem to have a short memory for in the current administration, to the point that they don't recognize that we have been and are currently in a war on terror.

Henceforth, we evolve from the first decade of the 21st Century with a charade of exponential decay of our Democracy with what appears to be the primary goal of President Obama's socialistic thesis of wealth redistribution with a plethora of programs to meet that objective.

Symbolism is an operative word in the Obama administration.

They wanted to see and project Gitmo as a symbol of what they wanted to strike as a significant difference from the Bush Administration, its interrogation techniques under an act of war and under the guidelines of the Geneva Convention. But Obama projected it as torture. So he wants to fulfill a campaign promise to shut down one of the most effective prisons we have for terrorists of war and send detainees to Illinois, all at taxpayer expense. One of the Obama objectives was to see that justice was served under US law.

The hypocrisy here is that some of these prisoners will never see the light of justice no matter where they will be held, all of which is contrary to Obama' righteous rhetoric.

There have been a number of hypocritical symbols within the past few years – let's examine some of these charades, try not to be too cynical about them, but question what happened to our values:

- Before former Vice President Al Gore lost his presidential bid to dangling chads in Florida, he invented the information highway, now known as the Internet. We don't hear him talking much about this today. No, today it's an inconvenient lie about global warming winning him the Nobel Peace Prize, while spilling carbon emissions from his fleet of jets, promoting science fiction around the world and becoming a billionaire.
- Then there is Ben Bernanke who wants to be reappointed as Chairman of the Federal Reserve, and was recently named man of the year by Time who encouraged the spending of $700 billion of taxpayer money for TARP, but does not want to see regulatory powers taken away from the Fed because it could lead to instability. Someone said that his concern over the Fed's role in maintaining financial stability is a bit like Hormel expressing concern over the treatment of cattle.
- Oh and there is Barney Frank who has always been fond of Fannie . . .Mae & Freddie . . . Mac giving out all those mortgages to people who couldn't afford them in the first place. Both need about a trillion more of a bailout to survive. Barney will be there for them.
- And how can we forget Tiger Woods in all of this symbolism of charades. He was named Athlete of the Decade by the Associated Press. It more appropriately might have been called 'swinger of the decade,' for a lifetime of dalliances.
- But it was President Barack Hussein Obama who walked away with the Nobel Peace Prize for Hope. He wasn't in

> **office but for a few months when the nomination for this award was submitted. He won the prize for being a hopeful peace president while conducting two wars, but with few achievements and lots of promises – few of which he has managed to deliver. Obama grows government, spends tax-payer monies, and runs banking and investment companies and the auto industry while pushing for health care reform and cap and trade, all with the blatant agenda of global redistribution of wealth.**

The two most significant pieces of legislation that moves towards this goal would include health care and cap and trade.

Obama is pushing hard for these bills, although the American public is against both by a margin of 2-1.

While the US contingent arrived in Copenhagen for the finality of a debate on climate warming appropriately a chilling blizzard swept over the two week conference.

It is interesting how this debate on global warming plays out. Two of the largest violators of carbon emissions happens to be China and India,

If a treaty were to be agreed upon, the US would have to borrow money from China to pay them for their contribution to alleged global warming with interest, because of our alleged contribution to global warming, pushing the US into further debt.

And with all of this nonsense going on Obama threatens the people of America, just before he takes off for his second junket to Copenhagen this month spilling more carbon emissions over an alleged warming climate, with bankruptcy if health care reform doesn't go through. We are already on the verge of bankruptcy with the current spending policies, what makes one think that if health care doesn't go through it will push our nation over the precipice.

It's a shame we don't have awards for charades of the decade. After all, this all happened in the first year of the Obama administration and we have three more years of charades before we can give the Tea Party a shot at straightening out this country.

LET'S VACATION AT THE WHITE HOUSE!

Washington DC (Storch Report) October 28, 2009 -- What do you think about a get-away?

What do you have in mind?

Well, I would like to do something different.

You mean you don't want to go on a cruise?

You got it!

How about we visit the White House?

What?

Let's discuss this. How much have we spent on our most expensive cruise?

Oh, about $40,000.

Well, I have a deal for you; we can probably negotiate a vacation over a period of time at the White House for about $30,400.

How does that work?

Well, as I understand it we have to get in touch with the Czar of Vacations at the White House.

We have to pledge $30,400 to the Democratic Party, you know, that's the maximum we can contribute and then we negotiate with the Czar as to what we want for the contribution.

You're good at that, look at the deals we got on our cruises, I always liked those Swedish valet's we had.

But, I'm new at this – what do I negotiate?

Well, for starters we request a night in the Lincoln bedroom, dinner with Barack and Michelle, breakfast in bed the next morning, a briefing on world and domestic affairs, lunch with the kids, a dog petting session with Bo and a visit to the veggie garden – plus a take-away of all the bathroom accoutrements – which will make nice souvenir talking points for our parties.

What else?

Well, I could probably get a round of golf out of this with Barack.

What would you talk about?

Oh, wealth distribution.

You, know we could probably get a bowling session for our grand kids with their children.

Our grand kids don't bowl!

Perhaps you could negotiate a basketball game for me with Obama, after all I did play college basketball. Maybe I could get a White House tee shirt.

You know, we would probably come home with some interesting souvenirs and experiences we could talk about, and you would have never-ending columns about someone you talk about endlessly, but not with admiration.

I don't know if this is for us?

You're probably right – you don't care much about dogs, so much for Bo, our kids don't bowl, I don't like his polices dealing with the economy, wealth redistribution, health care and we are not in sync with Marxism or socialism – why don't we take a cruise!

LIFE IS NOTHING BUT A PROMISE – THEN YOU GET A PRIZE

Washington DC (Storch Report) October 9, 2009 -- I always wanted to be a Major League Baseball player.

I didn't know all that it would take was a promise that I could do it.

I always dreamed to be a hero to someone.

I didn't know all it would take was a promise that I could fulfill that dream.

I always wanted to be a good student.

I didn't realize all it would take was a promise that I would be one.

I always wanted to be a success in life.

I didn't know that all it would take was a promise.

I always wanted to be a great writer.

I didn't know all it would take was a promise that I would be one.

I always wanted to have great friends.

I didn't know that all it would take was a promise that I would be one.

I always wanted to be a good father and husband.

I didn't know all it would take was a promise to be one.

Oh, but I found out today that promises are far greater than achievements.

I guess it was my parents that let me down.

They delivered some values that I thought were what life was about. Like, be true to thine own self. Be honest, work hard, pay your dues and you will achieve your rewards.

I knew at the time that advice seemed to be the hard way. But I bought into it because it made sense.

But today I found out that you can reach life's achievements with promises, a much easier way to receive rewards.

Well, you need a few electronic things to do it today, which didn't exist in my time, like a teleprompter. You first of all have to be a minority, black would be preferable, and speak in sentences that end with short cryptic words.

Most of what you speak must be in promises, with apologizes for the past which you inherited.

It is then that you reap the rewards.

And, you will find that it comes easy – that is if you understand global left wing politics.

I have packed up most of my prizes of achievement, boxed them and put them in a shed on my property for my children to wonder about.

I didn't make many promises, and today I feel somewhat like a failure.

A NEED TO BURY THE NEWS

Washington DC (Storch Report) August 25, 2009 -- Chief of Staff Raham Emanuel had his daily meeting with President Obama last Friday, prior to the president's departure for his vacation on Martha's Vineyard, and the subject was how to bury bad news.

"As you know Mr. President our 10-year projection of the national deficit is $9 trillion, $2 trillion off of our original projection, and I think we need to bury this story along with the negative news on health care reform coming out of town hall meetings," Emanuel said.

"What do you suggest?"

"Well, Mr. President, let's leak the new projected numbers at 5PM this evening after the market closes and let's hope the story dies over the weekend. Then I would suggest we pass along some ground rules to the press pool covering your vacation."

"What do you have in mind?"

"Let's suggest the media relax, walk the beach, leave the kids alone . . . and if they don't follow the rules, throw them out of the pool."

"Okay, what else?"

"On Monday we get Attorney General Eric Holder to name a federal prosecutor to examine abuse of prisoners held by the CIA, after releasing the report detailing abuses inside the CIA. This should take health care reform off of page one. Now, I know you

said you want to look ahead, and you can hold your position on this, but it's a way for us to bash Bush again and let Holder take the heat."

"That sounds good Raham."

"Then on Tuesday you rename Bernanke for a second 4-year term to the Fed, this should soften the market reaction to the $9 trillion deficit projection slated to be officially announced later in the day. I would suggest you then fade onto the golf course for a few rounds, go out to a local restaurant. This should take the hot topics off the table for the press and then we get back to business as usual next week."

"Raham, I always did like the way you think."

OBAMA'S DREAM OF 'KINJA'

Aboard Air Force One (Storch Report) July 11, 2009 -- Air Force One was flying smoothly at 35,000 feet on its way to Ghana, Western Africa and the President just finished his dry martini – shaken not stirred – and retired to his suite.

The kids were asleep in their room in their J. Crew trench coats – they liked them so much they wouldn't take them off when they went to bed.

Michelle was sound asleep in her J. Crew negligee. The first family was returning from the G-8 meeting in Italy with a stopover in Ghana, Africa.

Between the soft purr of Air Force One's jets and the martini, Obama quickly fell into the Rem zone of the sleep pattern.

A voice seemed to come through the clouds saying, "Speak it and they will believe . . . speak it and they will believe." Intermittently a soft voice kept repeating "Kinja, Kinja." Then the words, "Speak it and they will believe."

Obama knew his teleprompter prowess and understood the 'speak it believe it message,' but what was 'Kinja?'

The voice was too soft to be Rev. Jeremiah Wright . . . but perhaps it was God or Allah? Or, could it be all three speaking in unison?

Hell, Obama thought, I haven't even picked a Church yet, and all three are talking to me?

Then he remembered, after all he did go to Harvard and was well read . . . "its Herman Wouk's book, "Don't Stop the Carnival."

It all began to come back in his dream, it was a fictional story about an island in the Caribbean called Amerigo, but the natives knew it as, 'Kinja' and continued to call it what it once was. They pronounced it Keen-ja.

Yes, the story began to return to his memory bank. There was this Jew boy from New York . . . a Broadway Press Agent, who had it with the rat race in Manhattan and went to Kinja to buy a hotel and live a life in Paradise.

His name was Norman Paperman and sure enough he bought his dream, a hotel called the Gulf Reef Club.

But on the Island of Amerigo there was Governor Sanders and he controlled everything and his relatives, who all reported into him, were in charge of any service a business or a hotel might need – even water. Norman was stymied at every move he made – he was living in Governor Sanders 'Kinja.'

Obama thought as the dream was playing out, sounds a little bit like my 30 Czars – but he quickly cast this analogy aside by rationalizing the clever move he made to sidestep the Constitution making these incestuous servants responsible to him, not to the Congress or the people.

He began to think of his first 100 days in office and what he had already accomplished, and it did remind him a bit of 'Kinja.'

He thought of his achievements: passing a $787 Billion stimulus bill, that no one in Congress had read, in record time; took over the financial institutions and banks, and as a bonus, became the Czar of Czars by taking over General Motors, which became Government Motors, and in doing so by-passed all Constitutional bankruptcy laws, gave the people a 60 percent share of the company in return for a $50 Billion loan that the people will never recover.

It was a pleasant and pleasing dream at this point. He went on to thinking about how he could level the playing field within his own 'Kinja', redistributing wealth, taking care of the unions and his supporters by providing stimulus money on a quid pro quo

basis. The voice kept resounding in the background, "Speak it and they will believe it." He was dreaming of a second stimulus, even though the unemployment rate was reaching 10 percent.

Now he thought if I can get the Climate Bill passed, which no one has read, and rush through the Health Care Reform Bill, I will have put the nail in the coffin and transformed Amergo to where I think it should be and I will have Norman Paperman in a place where everyone else is.

He thought of the Bible at this point and Mark. He remembered something about Mark and a passage that said we will pay all men equally, if they work one hour, a half-day or a full day. They will all get the same pay. And that seemed to be fair . . . after all it came from the Bible.

But then within his own dream he had a stream of consciousness. "Oh, fathers I have sinned." He didn't know for sure if he was talking to God, Allah or Rev Wright. "Forgive me for looking at that young Brazilian girls' butt at the G-8 photo-op. I was on my way to picking up a dime to help in our stimulus package, and there it was."

The trio of voices spoke through a sun-lit cloud and said in unison, "It's all right you were in Berlusconi country and that's the way it's done there, after all it is Italy and that's where the Pope resides . . . and, as you know, he is all forgiving"

Obama wanted to continue with this pleasant dream, but it was then that Michelle rubbed against him in her J. Crew negligee and said, "We are landing soon in your home, dear."

"Oh, I'm sorry, Michelle . . . I was dreaming."

"Yes, I know . . . Was it pleasant?"

"Oh, yes."

"What was the outcome?"

"Oh, I don't know, you woke me too soon!"

WHEN THE REFRIGERATOR LIGHT WENT ON AND OBAMA LOOKED FOR THE TELEPROMPTERS

Washington DC (Storch Report) June 18, 2009 -- Michele are you awake? Obama asked the first lady?

"I am now 'O'"

"I feel like a bite to eat, would you like something from the fridge?"

"No 'O', I'm fine."

"Do you think the secret service follows me late at night to the kitchen?"

"I'll bet they do, with their jammies on and an ear piece."

"Well I'm going to try this out, I'm hungry for something."

Obama makes his way to the White House kitchen and sure enough a secret service agent in Washington Redskins jammies follows him to the kitchen.

Obama opens the refrigerator looking for a snack. The light goes on and he immediately looks for the Teleprompters to deliver a message. He doesn't see any and turns around and sees a secret service agent in his jammies.

The secret service agent says, "Mr. President may I help you?"

"Yes the President says, get me Gibbs on the phone, I want to know why the teleprompters were not here when the lights went on."

The agent pushed some buttons on his ear piece and a telephone rang in the kitchen and Gibbs was on the phone. The President answered.

"Yes Mr. President how can I be of help?" Gibbs said.

"Well, Gibbs the lights went on in the kitchen refrigerator and there were no Teleprompters there for me to deliver my message?"

"Mr. President, we didn't have any media interviews scheduled for 2 AM this morning."

"Oh, 'O' says. Perhaps we should talk in the morning to see if I'm being overexposed."

"I'll call to get on your schedule for a morning meeting," Gibbs said.

"Thanks," 'O' said, see you in the morning"

The President went back to bed after some smoked salmon.

Michelle was sound asleep.

The next morning the President had an early morning meeting with Gibbs and asked him very frankly, "Am I over exposed?"

"Well, Mr. President – we are doing very well in delivering our messages – the world loves you," Gibbs said.

"No, No, Gibbs cut to the chase - what's being said on the blogs?"

"Well, Mr. President, as you know we monitor Twitter and Facebook and there are some out there that believe that you want everyone to admire and worship you. They say that's what narcissists do, and if you really want the facts some have called you a 'pumpkin head'.

"Wow that's pretty strong Gibbs". "What else have you got?"

"Well, Mr. President, there are some out there that say you haven't figured out that the campaign is over. That you have low self-esteem issues and that you know you're screwing up so bad that you constantly need to be on TV to try to keep selling crap that people will buy. They think that you think you are our supreme

leader. They think that you deflect people's attention away from what's really going on in the world by being distracted by your charisma. They say it's in your teleprompter's contract," Gibbs reported.

The President got up and Gibbs said, "Where are you going Mr. President and what have you got in your hand?"

"Oh, Gibbs, I'll be right back – I'm just going to take a potty break and this is an Amazon Kindle — I'm just going to check out your report."

LET NOT YOUR HEART BE TROUBLED FOR OBAMA HAS A WEBSITE FOR OUR ECONOMIC WOES

Washington DC (Storch Report) March 31, 2009 --I really thought that when I reached this stage of my life, you know those golden years, when you have achieved your goals to the best of your ability and you're on the downside of the upside of life you wouldn't be moving to a state of economic depression because you're estate was devalued by some fifty percent. But I was comforted yesterday when our spending Messiah, President Barack Obama came through with a government website entitled "Getting through Tough Economic Times" and I thought 'hallelujah', 'Let not my heart be troubled.'

I thought from my profound biblical background this makes a lot of sense. He is my President and he really cares for me. I know that he inherited a lot and he wants me to believe that he has a lot on his plate to deal with. But with all of this, and despite his Trillions of spending, his socialistic policies, the taxes he is going to deliver to all of us, even me in my golden years, and the fact that he is going to be CEO of Corporate America in order to save our economy and destroy capitalism – he has convinced me that he cares about me because he developed a website anticipating my economic depression in these difficult times.

So, I went to the website to not allow my heart to be troubled.

What I found was the equivalent of a patient package insert that I might receive from the pharmacy for the drugs that I take.

There was an Eagle on the top of the page and that was comforting, but then the opening comments were somewhat disconcerting, "This guide provides practical advice on how to deal with the effects financial difficulties can have on your physical and mental health – it covers: possible health risks, warning signs, managing stress, getting help, suicide warning signs, other steps you can take."

I thought to myself that I have taken serious prescription drugs with fewer side effects. But then they told me what the possible health risks that I might face and they listed, depression, anxiety, compulsive behaviors (over-eating, excessive gambling, spending, etc.), and substance abuse.

Now just like those patient package inserts – that you should really read– there were warning signs. They talked about my financial problems affecting my emotional or mental well-being. The signs were persistent sadness/crying; excessive anxiety; lack of sleep/constant fatigue; excessive irritability/anger; increased drinking; illicit drug use, including misuse of medications; difficulty paying attention or staying focused; apathy - not caring about things that are usually important to you and not being able to function as well at work, school or home.

Now I worked in the pharmaceutical industry for decades and never remembered a drug with these kinds of side effects. And it is interesting to note, from my perspective of my golden years, they don't cover contraindications. What could these be? Perhaps only Obama knows.

Now they talk about managing stress and this is pap. They talk about getting help, mostly from agencies that no longer have the money to give it and they suggest you seek out Federal and state government aid.

This all is a pretty big pill to swallow – perhaps we should get rid of the pill and avoid the side effects and 'Let not our heart to be troubled.'

ARMS . . . A PART OF THE FEMALE ANATOMY WE DIDN'T LOOK AT FIRST UNTIL MICHELLE OBAMA BECAME FIRST LADY

Washington DC (Storch Report) March 1, 2009 -- Sleeveless in February was a fashion no, no until first lady Michelle Obama introduced her long lanky toned arms to the Nation last week when President Obama addressed Congress for the first time.

This certainly is a 'change' the first lady brought to Washington DC; bringing overwhelming attention to her gazelle-like toned arms that some are calling sexy and putting hers in a class with "Madonna arms" and "Kelly Ripa arms" to the point where some women are calling on physical trainers to give them "Obama arms."

Now a lot has been written about man's instincts about women. Some go as far as to call us animals and others say, more accurately, we are "loons."

Many female authors blame it all on our genes. J. Kearns in an essay on How Men Choose Women, said "Men want to look. First, foremost and always, men are visual. Men's eyes are always wandering, seeking out that which they could and would impregnate." She says, "Why is this so, Mr. Darwin? Well, it's because the genes that triggered that kind of behavior had the best chance of survival down through the ages until all the men who were left had those genes."

The fact is men can't help looking, even happily married men. Former President Jimmy Carter, while in office, admitted that he too "had lust."

However, the list of items that a male is usually attracted to in the female anatomy, are hooters, butts and gams . . . not arms.

Now some of us are leg men, breast men and butt men, and the order may very well vary for each of us. Others want the physical combination of all three along with a pretty face.

Now it is true that we would prefer toned arms over bat wings, but for our genes to get excited over lanky well-toned arms when there is so much more . . . I just don't know.

Different men like completely different bodies. Some like slender, athletic female figures. Some like the model type, others with riper curves. And, there was that artist who painted those larger women, who might be called obese today, but were "Rubenesque" yesterday.

If there are "Obama arms" could there be "Rubenesque arms" that might come into vogue?

I think it is time for the lyricists and song writers to put pen to paper and develop a song entitled Those Sexy Arms. Perhaps I can give the lyricist a clue and the song writer can develop a melody . . . "Wrap those well-toned lanky "Obama arms" around this svelte "ripped" body once, twice three times . . ."

If Barack can continue to 'sweet talk' us into a spending Depression, Michelle capture us with her 'well-toned sexy arms' and Rush Limbaugh convince us God wants to be him, I'm sure we can be distracted enough to get through these uplifting times.

While arms may be in and becomes the new fashion female part of the anatomy of today, give me the old fashion hooters, butts and gams.

MR. SMITH GOES TO WASHINGTON . . . AGAIN!

Washington DC (Storch Report) February 15, 2009 -- Mr. Thaddeus Smith was an unlikely winner to a US Senate seat from Apalachicola Florida, running as a Democrat and swept into office by the Obama mania of 2008.

He was as surprised as everyone else, when in January of 2009 he found himself in the freshman class of the United States Senate.

Within 20 days in office he was on a ride he never experienced in Disney World.

Riding a high on the heels of the inauguration ceremonies and then being welcomed into the Senate by House leader Nancy Pelosi, (D-Ca) and Senate leader Harry Reid (D-NV) and riding a crest of "Change" which was the theme of the Obama campaign along with bringing "Bipartisanship" back to DC, Thaddeus' chest was bursting with pride.

He quietly thought to himself, Mr. Smith returns to Washington... Again!

After his swearing in ceremonies, he met with Pelosi and Reid and they graciously welcomed him to Congress. They quickly told him that the President wanted to immediately pass a stimulus bill to infuse the economy with spending due to the dire straits the economy was in that they inherited from the Bush administration.

They unabashedly told him as a Democrat and as a freshman Senator he would need to fall in line quickly and vote for a package that would probably be in the range of $800 billion, a figure that Thaddeus couldn't comprehend coming from Apalachicola.

He said he would promise to cooperate being a good Democrat, but that he would have to look at the specifics of the bill in order to be responsible to his constituents from the State of Florida.

Then within a fast-past 20 days of conference meetings on the House side and likewise on the Senate side, none of which he was part of, the House passed a stimulus bill — which was described by many as a spending bill — with no Republican votes.

The Bill went to the Senate, and they paired it back a bit adding some of their own spending and convinced three defectors from the Republican Party to support the bill getting more than 60 votes to avoid a filibuster. Sen. Thaddeus Smith voted against the bill.

The bill went into joint conference committee meetings for negotiations and settlement. Sen. Smith was not part of the process. It passed the House with no Republican support. It then went to the Senate for a vote.

Before the vote Reid and Pelosi called Sen. Smith into a meeting for a heart to heart talk.

"Sen. Smith, we need your vote on this stimulus package," said Reid.

"Harry, in good conscious, I can't vote for what appears to be a spending bill not a stimulus bill," said Smith.

"I came to Washington expecting "Change" and "Bipartisanship" and what I find is the same old same old.

"This is a spending bill, with only 23% stimulus and 73% spending, and you two are the worst Hypocrites in the Congress.

"You Harry, want a Reid railway from LA to Las Vegas to the tune of $8 billion... to what, take money out of the pockets of our citizens?

"And you Nancy want $30 million for a mouse in some eco-protected land in San Francisco?

"As for tax breaks in an economic crisis, you are going to give back to each citizen $13 a week — what to buy a Big Mac?

"And as for Obama and all of his wonderful "Change" and denunciation of lobbyists, he puts two into two high level positions and names three tax evaders to Cabinet positions, two of which had to withdraw and he still can't find a Secretary of Commerce after two withdrew their nomination, one because he was indicted by a Federal Grand Jury and the other over principals and ethics.

"On top of all of this, you give me less than 24 hours to read a $787 billion bill of 1,000 pages, with all kind of phantom proposals, under hidden codes, and you want my yes vote?

"You have my "no" vote, you're not going to manipulate this Senator", Harry, Nancy.

"Sen. Smith, perhaps you should once again view, "Mr. Smith Goes to Washington", and live in your fantasy world. We here in Washington live in reality," said Sen. Reid.

AT LAST I CAN DANCE TO 'AT LAST' 10 INAUGURAL BALLS IN A ROW

Washington DC (Storch Report) January 21, 2009 -- What wasn't revealed during the 10 Inaugural Balls the Obama's attended this evening was what they said to each other while they were dancing to the same song, 'At Last.' Now it can be disclosed:

President: "What do you think dear, am I getting better on the dance floor?"

First Lady: "Well you're better Barack at the fifth dance than you we're on the first. And, very frankly you're better at kissing as the Balls go on, especially than you were at bowling.

President: "Michelle, your dress seems to be a little long and it impedes my moves.

First Lady: "My gown seems to have a long train that's getting in the way."

President: "Well, my dear, I thought we left the train a few days ago."

First Lady: "Very funny dear."

President: "Next time, I think you should wear a short cocktail gown, I like your legs."

First Lady: "Well, dear just keep in mind you've got more on your agenda tomorrow than my legs."

President: "You're right; I've got a basketball game at 6 AM. Michelle, I think we've got our favorite song down on the dance floor.

First Lady: "Barack, I think you have achieved your goal, 'At Last.'

NEW YEAR'S DAY BREAKFAST AT THE BLAGOJEVICH'S

Chicago (Storch Report) January 1, 2009 -- Can you imagine breakfast at the Blagojevich's home on the first day of the New Year?

Patty: "Well Rod what do you think we face this year?

Rod: "Oh, It will be a lot like last year . . . politics as usual. As I promised the people of Illinois, I will 'fight, fight, and fight.'"

Patty: "Rod, I must admit that was a clever move on your part to appoint Roland Burris to fill Obama's Senate seat."

Rod: "Thanks honey. You see it serves several purposes, as Governor of the state of Illinois I have a responsibility to the people to continue to do my job despite the alleged charges against me of corruption, furthermore I have injected the race card by appointing an Afro American to fill an Afro American's seat and this should give pause to those (bleeping) senators in Congress who want to block any nomination I make. We'll take the nomination to the Supreme Court if necessary. And lastly, it's a distraction against the issues surrounding me."

Patty: "You certainly have big Cajon's, dear."

Rod: "Well you have to, after all I am all but convicted in the court of public opinion before I have been indicted and had a fair trial in the court of justice. And on top of this, the Illinois legislature wants to impeach me without a fair trial."

Patty: What do you think Patrick Fitzgerald's got?"

Rod: "That (bleeping) guy has nothing but words. I did nothing wrong. We'll handle this the same way Bill Clinton handled the Monica Lewinsky affair. After all, 'What is the definition of is?' "They've got nothing but words and as you well know words have many meanings."

Patty: "What if this all goes down, what's your ace in the hole?"

Rod: "That's easy, if they really want me out of the Governor's office we'll put the pressure on for an Obama pardon in exchange for my resignation."

Patty: "Then what will we do?"

Rod: "We'll come back just as Richard Nixon did . . . please pass me the scrambled eggs, Patty."

HUMOR A CRITERIA FOR FUTURE PRESIDENTIAL DEBATES

Washington DC (Storch Report) – October 17, 2008 -- The Commission on Presidential Debates met today and decided that all future Presidential debate candidates would have to respond to questions as to why they should be president and how they would deal with the critical issues of our nation with humor, satire and cynicism.

After all if it's going to take us two years to elect a president of this republic, the electorate should at least be entertained, was the conclusion of the Commission.

I couldn't agree with the Commission more after examining the transcript. We could immediately measure the winner or loser of a debate with a laugh-a-meter. We wouldn't need polls; we could register audience reactions at the forum along with Neilson ratings of TV audience reactions.

Obama and McCain proved the Commission's decision when they scored more points against each other with humor, satire and cynicism in one evening of fun than they did in three presidential debates.

McCain said, "Events are moving fast in my campaign. And, yes, it's true that this morning I dismissed my entire team of senior advisers. All of these positions will now be held by a man named, "Joe the Plumber."

Obama said in the spirit of full disclosure, there are a few October surprises you'll be finding out about in the coming weeks. "First of all, my middle name is not what you think. It's actually Steve. That's right. Barack Steve Obama."

McCain said the Obama campaign claims that this honest, hardworking small businessman could not possibly have enough income to face a tax increase under the Obama plan. "What they don't know is, "Joe the Plumber" recently signed a very lucrative contract with a wealthy couple to handle all the work on all seven of their houses.

Obama tried to answer who he is. He said, "Contrary to the rumors you have heard, I was not born in a manger.

"I was born on Krypton and sent here by my father Jerel to save the Planet Earth."

McCain tried to make the point that this campaign needed the common touch of a working man. "After all, it began so long ago with the heralded arrival of a man known to Oprah Winfrey as, "The One." Being a friend and colleague of Barack, I just called him "that one."

"And he – my friends, he doesn't mind at all. In fact, he even has a pet name for me – "George Bush."

Obama responded, "Many of you – many of you know that I got my name, Barack, from my father. What you may not know is Barack is actually Swahili for "That One."

"And I got my middle name from somebody who obviously didn't think I'd ever run for president.

"If I had to name my greatest strength, I guess it would be my humility.

"Greatest weakness, it's possible that I'm a little too awesome."

McCain feeling somewhat out of place in a Manhattan hotel filled with Democrats said," There are signs of home even in the most unexpected places – even in this room full of proud Manhattan Democrats. I can't – I can't shake that feeling that some people here are pulling for me.

"I'm delighted to see you here tonight, Hillary."

Obama talking about his associations, said "Here's another revelation, John McCain is on to something. There was a point in my life when I started palling around with a pretty ugly crowd. I've got to be honest; these guys were serious dead beats. They were low lives, unrepentant, no-good punks.

"That's right. I've been a member of the United States Senate.

"Come to think of it, John, I swear I saw you at one of our meetings."

Taking a poke at the media, McCain said, "My old friend and Green Room pal Chris Matthews used to like me, but he found somebody new – somebody who opened his eyes, somebody who gave him a thrill up his leg.

"And we've talked about it. I told him maverick I can do, but messiah is above my pay grade.

"You know, it's going to be a long, long night MSNBC if I manage to pull this thing off."

And so a vote for humor.

I HAD A BAD DREAM LAST NIGHT . . . OBAMA WAS PRESIDENT

Washington DC (Storch Report) October 5, 2008 -- A few days after the inauguration Barack Obama, the first black President of the United States, held a meeting in the Oval office on three critical issues facing America, the economy, the Iraq war and terrorism.

Present for this meeting were three Cabinet members, and their assistants all close friends and some advisors to the President during his presidential campaign: Franklin Raines, Secretary of the Treasury and former Chairman and Chief Executive Officer of Fannie Mae; Tony Rezko, Secretary Department of Defense, and convicted felon; William Ayers, Secretary of Homeland Security, and former terrorist with the Weathermen, who threatened to blow up the Pentagon.

Also at the meeting were Under Secretaries to the Cabinet members: Under Secretary of the Treasury, Tim Howard, former Chief Financial Officer of Fannie Mae; Bernadine Dohrn Under Secretary of Defense and a former Weathermen terrorist with William Ayers and Rev. Jeremiah Wright Jr. Undersecretary of Homeland Security, who was known for finding Jesus for our President and his classic statement from the pulpit, "God Damn America"

It was a stalwart collection of key cabinet members brought together to deal with key critical issues facing the future of

America and each was asked to use their expertise and past 'successful' accomplishments to deal with future problems.

Obama called the meeting to order reminding everyone how tough he is, having come from Chicago and surviving the most vitriolic national election campaign ever.

He pointed out that there were more murders in Chicago in the last six months than in Iraq, 292 to 221, giving him the experience to execute a rapid withdrawal of our troops from a place they shouldn't have been in the first place.

He pointed to the importance of a Democratic controlled congress. "Just look at what we did in Chicago, with me as senator, along with Dick Durbin, Rep. Jesse Jackson Jr., Gov Rod Blogojevich, House leader Mike Madigan, Atty. Gen. Lisa Madigan, Mayor Richard Daley, all Democrats."

Then Barack reviewed the record in Chicago, the State pension fund was $44 billion in debt, worst in the country. Cook County sales tax 10.25%, highest in the country and the Chicago school system one of the worst in the country. Obama then said, "This is the political culture that we can bring to the United States."

He then said to each of his Cabinet members that he was confident that he had appointed the appropriate persons, based upon their past accomplishments, to a leadership role to face these three critical issues.

It was then that I woke up from a bad dream, in a cold sweat.

OBAMA FLOAT'S RESIGNATION TO BIDEN; HILLARY IN WINGS?

Washington DC (Storch Report) September 22, 2008 -- The morning after Sarah Palin drew some 60,000 persons to a rally at The Villages outside of Orlando Florida yesterday, Barack Obama sat down with Joe Biden to discuss some future strategy.

According to sources inside the Obama campaign, the conversations went something like this:

"Joe as you know this Palin phenomenon is gaining momentum. I don't know if you saw it or not but she drew 60,000 at The Villages out of 90,000 residents and the Palin dolls are selling off the shelves. What we need Joe is Plan B."

"Barack what is it that you are suggesting?"

"Well Joe I'm not suggesting anything at this point, but I think we need to have a strategy if things begin to go south."

"You know Joe; you yourself said during this campaign that Hillary Clinton would have been a better selection than you."

"But Barack that was just political rhetoric."

"Well Joe, I guess the question here is whether you will do the best thing for your country if it becomes necessary?"

"You know I will do that, what do you have in mind."

"Well our strategists have come up with Plan B. We will assess how well you do against Palin after the Vice Presidential Debates

on October 2. If you do well and the polls reflect this, we will stay the course. However, if we go down in the polls, the strategists are suggesting that you resign due to health problems.

"As you know, historically this would not be an unprecedented move, VP nominee; Tom Eagleton resigned due to health problems."

"But Barack, he resigned due to mental health problems . . . I don't have any mental health problems."

"Joe, let's not split hairs you have had neurological disease, both conditions fall in the same medical category. You have had surgery for two aneurysms and after the last one you didn't return to the Senate until seven months after diagnosis."

"Barack, do you think the public is not going to see this for what it is a grand manipulative maneuver?"

"I don't know Joe, it seems quite credible to me. I mean after all, Congresswoman Stephanie Tubbs Jones just recently died of a ruptured brain aneurysm. Furthermore it is well known in medical circles that patients with a history of brain aneurysms can sometimes develop new ones. By the way Joe, did you know that in our history seven Vice Presidents died in office?

"Joe, the plan would be — that is if we had to execute this strategy — that you would resign on October 5. We would promote you as the patriot you are and you would be portrayed as a hero who stepped up to the plate for his country and his party. As for the campaign, it is anticipated that we would get a major bump in the polls, pick-up 18 million of Hillary's votes and it would probably set-up the Obama-Clinton ticket for a major election landslide."

"Think about it Joe, we are not going to rush into any decisions . . . it is just an option."

PACKAGING PALIN

Manasota Key FL (Storch Report) September 8, 2008 -- Somehow I feel a bit like Rodney Dangerfield when he was alive. He, as you know, built a comic career out of 'not getting any respect.'

Recently I just changed my look; I ordered some new eyeglasses, handmade Barrister Liberty, made in England, with Transition Anti-Glare lenses with a frame color of amber Havana.

On my first night out with close friends, no one noticed my new glasses.

Some six years ago I was tired of my comb-over hair look, so I shaved it all off the evening of a Valentine's day party, took some lollypops' with me and handed them out to everyone who asked me about my hair, or lack thereof.

They all went home that evening believing that I was going through chemo therapy.

But now a little over a week after being a virtual unknown, Vice Presidential nominee Alaska Gov. Sarah Palin pops on to the political scene and has stolen the campaign's style spotlight, causing a run on Kawasaki 704 eyeglass frames and upswept hairstyles.

Somehow, I think you can see how I feel a bit like Rodney.

Now Sarah did this with a lot of competition. There was Sen. Hillary Rodham Clinton, you remember her don't you? She was that Democratic candidate running against Obama, who introduced those gender-neutral pantsuits and of course there was

Cindy McCain's $300,000 Oscar de la Renta-and-diamond convention outfit and Michelle Obama's throwback to Jackie O. shift dresses.

But no one captured the style-minded country like Sarah Palin.

After all I didn't want to capture the country, I just wanted to be noticed among some unknowns who were known to me – but all they thought was that I was sick despite my Tele Zavala's lollypop move.

Now you can't ignore the Palin style strategy, it is quite clever. After all the beauty queen turned politician knows how to play up her sexuality. She knows she's a trophy; she wears skirts that are form-fitting and often goes without stockings. The night of the convention she wore a black satin jacket that showed just enough cleavage to make it sexy.

She once said she was trying to be "as frumpy as I could by wearing my hair on top of my head and these schoolmarm glasses" so that I could get to the real business of governing and shooting caribou.

That's exactly what I did when I shaved my head, it doesn't take me long to get ready to go to a Valentine's party.

There will always be those that will question whether style is a substitute for substance.

All that's left for me now, is upswept eyebrows!

THE DREAM TICKET, BARACK & SARAH?

Washington DC (Storch Report) September 3, 2008 -- With all the flack that's flying around during this Presidential campaign, especially over Gov. Sarah Palin's selection as the GOP nominee for Vice President, I thought of a way we might resolve this media racist/sexist personal attack-dog mentality – why don't we merge the two young candidates, Barack and Sarah, elect them to office, and send John and Joe to the early bird special at a Florida assisted living facility?

After all, we are really not going to get change from John and Joe, who nap every afternoon, our hope is in a Barack and Sarah ticket where inexperience abounds and change will take place by mere trial and error.

This dream ticket would be the first of firsts: the first black president; the first female vice president; the first inexperienced team leading the US; the first president born to a mother of 18; the first VP with five children, one of which is a teen who is pregnant; the first president who associates with felons and who has had a minister that helped him find Jesus, but denounces the US; the first VP whose husband is a blue collar worker and has been arrested on a DUI; the first president who was associated with a Weatherman terrorist and was raised a Muslim; the first VP whose husband is a snowboard race champion in Alaska; the first president who plays basketball; the first VP who was a point guard and hunts the wilds

of Alaska for bear; the first handsome president with big ears, and the first VP who was a beauty pageant winner.

Aren't these the attributes that we are looking for in a dream ticket? It's important the president and the vice president show that they are human so they can relate to the common man. It is important they make the mistakes we see in all families, after all how else can we relate to them?

Most of us are not interested in resolving issues such as the energy crisis, the economy, ending the war in Iraq, what judges we will name to the Supreme Court, prochoice or prolife, gun control, homosexual marriage, tax increase, reform social security, capital gains tax, dividend tax, income tax and inheritance tax.

A Barack, Sarah ticket will provide the fodder for the grocery store tabloids, what more could we ask for?

SPITTING & BASEBALL

Manasota Key FL (Storch Report) August 19, 2008 -- I have been planning to write a column on Spitting & Baseball for some time now, but after watching this evening's game between the Tampa Bay Rays and the Los Angeles Angels (TB 4 LA 2) the spitting issue seemed to come more into focus.

There was an incident at first base after B.J. Upton hit an infield ground ball ran to first base and the Angels overthrew first base, a runner scored from third Upton was safe at first and then somehow, beyond belief and replay, the umpire called Upton out for what he perceived to be a turn to second base after the first baseman touched him while he was to the right of the foul line.

Tampa Bay's manager Joe Madden went ballistic, charged the umpire with vitriolic expletives and was eventually thrown out of the ballgame. What followed was as interesting as the inexcusable call. Video cameras captured the short spectacled umpire, spitting fast balls between his teeth.

The cameras then focused on B.J. Upton in the dugout spitting the same sputum fast balls over the railing.

I never understood what all this spitting was about in baseball. I played a lot of baseball, but was never very good at spitting. Perhaps that is why I didn't make the show.

I also never realized that spitting was an integral part of the game; I always thought it had something to do with hitting, throwing and catching the ball.

After all spitting really doesn't exist in other sports.

Can you imagine an Olympic competitor in ping pong spitting on the floor, or a basketball player doing the same? We don't even have spitting in tennis by players or umpires, and that is an outdoor sport.

It seems to me that owners of major league franchises should insure the fans that the field is sprayed with Lysol before and after games with all this spitting going on.

Now we know that chewing tobacco has been a big part of the game for years with both players, managers and umpires, perhaps that is why the infield has that brown cast.

Some ballplayers chew bubble gum and blow bubbles, others chew slippery elm and they all spit.

Ballplayers spit better than the average population, some probably spit knuckle balls.

No one has ever gotten down to the real reason for spitting in baseball, but I saw all the reasons this evening, the umpire making a bad call knew he was wrong and was spitting out of guilt, Upton was spitting out of frustration for the bad call and all the other ballplayers spit because they grab their crotch too often.

FICKLE FAY FIZZLES

Manasota Key FL (Storch Report) August 19, 2008 -- I live in one of the worst places to be when a tropical storm approaches, a barrier reef in the Gulf of Mexico.

They built up my expectations as Fay approached, as they always do when a tropical storm forms and heads towards Florida.

They said Fay would possibly reach a category 1 or 2 at the most. So when I awoke this morning my expectations were to see high seas in the Gulf with water coming up to my rip rap and winds whipping my palm trees around violently.

Instead I saw calm seas and very little wind; in fact I've played golf in more treacherous weather.

I picked up our local paper, the Sarasota Herald Tribune, and here were some of the headlines: 'Fay aims for mainland after hitting the keys'; 'Region is battened down and closed for the duration'; Senior care centers and hospitals ready for the worst'; 'Some balk at move to shelters'; Schools are closed for the day'; 'Charlotte nervous as storm approaches'; 'Playing it safe inside your home'; 'Don't let your guard down'; Tips on food and water'; 'Taking care of damage in your yard'; 'A methodical cleanup'.

And, all of this storm hype was just as bad on radio and TV. There was that typical standup reporter at Fisherman's Village in Punta Gorda, where Charley came through five years ago and devastated the community and all he really could talk about, you got

it, was Charley. He would have needed an airboat to create wind and the rain wasn't cooperating either.

Now, I didn't take any of this lightly. I tucked all my outdoor furniture away so it would not become a flying missile, put my golf cart in the garage along with my cars, doubled the lines on my boat, and checked my flashlights and battery operated radio to see that they were working.

The day before the storm was to arrive I called my doctor to change an appointment next month only to find out I was talking to an answering service; they had shut down the office and wouldn't reopen for four days.

You see, here in Florida work stops for just about any reason, especially happy hour, but a tropical storm is one of the best of all reasons to have an extended happy hour.

Fickle Fay fizzled, but I guess merchants sold some batteries, water and plywood boards and the local bars are doing well.

Now all I have to do is undo what I did to prepare for Fay.

Oh, I am not unhappy that the Storm wasn't what was predicted, it's my expectations that I now have to deal with, much like my banker who called the other day to tell me he found a 4.75% CD, only to call me back and tell me he made a mistake, it was only 3.75%.

HOW WOULD YOU LIKE YOUR ICE?

Manasota Key Fl (Storch Report) August 11, 2008 -- "I'll have a Tanqueray gin on the rocks."

"How would you like your ice?" Fragmented, nugget or cubed, shaved, dimpled on the ends with or without bubbles or mystically clear?"

"Hell, my friend, I just want a drink that's cold . . . I don't want to buy a tie."

For ice aficionados this sort of dialog is not that far off the mark.

I never thought much about ice until I didn't have enough of it.

This often occurs in Europe; they not only skimp on the booze but most often the ice.

Some say its conservation, but others say the Europeans do not want to water down their alcohol.

Whatever it is, here in the United States there is a trend toward gourmet cubes. Some individuals go so far as BYOI when going to a party . . . that's bring your own ice, if you didn't figure it out before I told you.

There is nothing worse than cloudy ice, or ice with bubbles in it, or for that matter ice from those waffle trays that have been so close to stored food they absorb the taste.

And then again it could be a sanitary thing rather than a snob thing.

The purity of ice was brought into focus a few years ago when a student here in Florida discovered that the water from toilets was purer than that from ice machines, some of which was contaminated with E. coli bacteria among other unsavory things.

You see this just proves that all ice is not equal. It may come from water, but where did the water come from and who touched the ice before it went into the glass and if it's cloudy or not crescent shaped it certainly didn't come from a gourmet ice machine.

After giving some thought to this ice thing and not being a snob about it all, but taking all issues into consideration, I thought I would make my cubes crystal clear out of Tanqueray gin, this would take care of the bacteria issue while resolving the European concerns of a watered down drink.

OBAMA'S WAILING WALL RUSE

Onboard Air Force One (Storch Report) July 30, 2008 -- Obama's low-key master strategist David Plouffe sat alongside Barack on the recent flight to the Middle East and said, "Barack I have a Wailing Wall of an idea. Now with all that you have on your plate for this trip, I don't want you to take your eye off the ball, but believe me this little side trip to the Wall will pay off big time."

"What's the idea," Obama asked.

"Well one evening while you are in Israel, you make an early morning visit to the Wailing Wall. There will be few people around and you pray and leave your handwritten prayer at the wall. We will see to it that a picture of you wearing a yamakai is taken. We will also see to it that a local newspaper picks up your prayer. Believe me, it will make the A wires of the Associated Press and be seen worldwide."

"But what would I say in my prayer?" Obama asks.

"Here it is. Very brief, says Plouffe, 'Lord – Protect my family and me.' We will put this on stationery from the King David hotel where you will be staying . . . it will look like an impromptu thing. The prayer will close with, 'Forgive me my sins, and help me guard against pride and despair. Give me the wisdom to do what is right and just. And make me an instrument of your will.'"

"Gee's," David, "that sounds great. Do you think we could ask God for a little help in becoming President of the United States?"

"Well, Barack, that's what we are doing but in a bit more subtle way."

"Oh, I see, we don't want to be blatant about it."

"Now let's think this through. As I understand this, the Wall which the Jews call the Western Wall, is the most sacred of places, because the temple itself was thought to be the place where God resides on earth. Praying here signifies being in the presence of the Divine. And as I understand, revealing your prayer is a sin?"

"That's right," Barack, "but that only applies to the Jews. And being that the world doesn't know whether you're a Christian, Muslim or Baptist, you get a free ride and we can get away with this."

"But, But you don't think we should ask God to make me President? After all Jews from all countries, and as well as tourists of other religious backgrounds, come to pray at the Wall, where it is said one immediately has the 'ear of God.' I would love to have the ear of God; perhaps we could make a TV commercial out of the event."

"Well, I don't think we should go that far."

"David, I understand there is a charge for slipping a prayer in-between the cracks of the Wall. Do you think our campaign can afford this?"

BEEP

Manasota Key Fl (Storch Report) July 8, 2008 -- It's about 3 AM now when I'm writing this piece because I can't sleep.

It all started about 1:30AM when I mistakenly turned over during a sound sleep.

My wife said to me, "did you hear that?"

"Did I hear what?"

"That beep."

"What beep?"

"Listen."

My wife is much like a raccoon, nocturnal. She is usually awake at this hour, counting sheep or beeps.

We both listened and about 5 minutes later there was a beep.

She said, "You think it's the fire alarm?"

I said no the fire alarm is hooked up to the electric system and doesn't have batteries that beep when they are low.

"It's probably one of your gadgets, like the driveway alert or the front door alert."

"Why does it always have to be one of my gadgets? You have gadgets that beep also. How about the microwave, or the electric range, or the dishwasher, the washing machine or your cell phone."

"This is like an Erma Bombeck story," I said to my wife. She buys old Bombeck books on e-bay.

One of her favorite stories was reading from the 'bottom of the cage.' This was when Bombeck's husband read to her what she already read. We do this; my wife gets the paper because she's the first one up. The paper isn't much of a paper and doesn't take long to read . . . it takes about five minutes and she can do this in between beeps. Then I get up and read to her what she already read . . . from the bottom of the cage.

"Did you hear that . . . there it goes again?"

"Well it's annoying."

"Not as annoying as you waking me up."

"We're going away in the morning and I don't want that thing beeping while we're gone."

"You won't hear it in the Virgin Islands," I said.

Well my wife got up and dressed, as she usually does at this hour, and went downstairs to read Erma Bombeck.

I told her to pull the front door alert from the receptacle to see if that would stop the beeping.

It did and she was right, it was one of my gadgets.

I can't sleep now, so I'm reading to you from the bottom of the cage.

"OH, WE'RE DOWN AT THE STORKNEST," SAID OSSIE THE OSPREY

Manasota Key Fl (Storch Report) April 27, 2008 -- Ossie the Osprey flew into an island of mangroves in Lemon Bay and settled down alongside Woody the Wood Stork.

"Hey, Ossie what have you been up to?"

"Oh, I've just been flying around trying to get away from the old lady."

"Where you hanging out these days?"

"Oh, we're down at the Storknest on Manasota Key."

"You're at the Storknest, I should be at Storknest — after all, I'm a Stork."

"Well we've been there some five years now; we've got a rooftop suite about 150 feet up in the air in a Norfolk Pine, with a great view of the Gulf of Mexico.

"I didn't even know that the people that own this place called it the Storknest until after I moved in.

"Where are you guys these days?"

"We're on the mainland at Boca Royale Country Club; the old lady doesn't like hurricanes."

"You should fly-by some day and I'll buy you a snapper. After lunch we can let the gals chat and we can go to my den, a matching Norfolk Pine which sits parallel to our home, and down a few."

"That sounds great Ossie."

Ossie and Woody go back a few years. They both went to Bird College together and discovered Manasota Key during a spring break.

Ossie found the Storknest through the internet, the guy that lives there is a blog.

He did a fly-by and found those two Norfolk Pines on an acre of land on the Gulf. He selected the left tree entering the walled compound and saw how the tree bifurcated at the top and quickly deducted from his engineering background that it was a perfect place for a nest.

Ossie knew the history of his family realizing that the Osprey's diet consists almost exclusively of fish and this location didn't require him to go far to provide for his family.

Knowing full well that it's his family's nature to mate for life he thought he should pick the location for his nest carefully – after all he heard somewhere here in Florida that it was location, location, location.

He checked out the tree carefully taking into account that he and his wife weigh between 3 and 4 lbs and have a wingspan of 5-6 feet and need an appropriate landing zone. He then had to take into consideration that mama was going to hatch two to four eggs and he wanted a nest that could house everyone at once.

He scouted the area for the appropriate materials for the nest and knew that he needed an abundance of sticks, driftwood and seaweed to be built in the fork of this tree in order to build a sturdy nest for the family, but one that was small enough to keep the family warm in chilly weather.

The Storknest was the place for Ossie and his mate.

A few weeks after Ossie flew into the mangroves and met Woody, Ossie was in his den, which also served as a sentry post for his home, and he saw Woody and his wife coming into the flight pattern. He took off to escort them into the nest.

They landed and with the appropriate bird perfunctory greetings behind them, Ossie said he was going out for the snapper he promised Woody.

Ossie was between 32 and 130 feet above the Gulf when he spotted his prey just offshore of the Storknest when he plunged feet first into the water his nostrils automatically closed, he clutched onto the snapper ascended quickly and during flight shifted the fish from a horizontal position to a vertical one to eliminate drag on takeoff.

Back at the nest the Osprey's and Stork's were finishing up lunch, when Ossie suggested to Woody that they retire to the Den in the other Norfolk Pine and have an after dinner drink.

"Hey, Ossie how are you getting along with your neighbor?"

"Oh, you mean the blog?"

"Yeh."

"Well, in the beginning we had a little trouble. I accidentally dropped a pretty good size snapper in the driveway. You see his garage sits right under our nest. The fish stuck to his tire and he didn't recognize it until the next morning when he opened the garage door.

"I guess the garage smelled pretty bad. Well that day he climbs the 150 feet to my penthouse suite and wants to charge me rent.

"I told him that if he didn't get out of my tree I would drop a dozen fish a day in his driveway. Then he started negotiating with me to go into business and he would sell the fish.

"I didn't hear from him again until he came up here again complaining about the kids pooping on his red tile roof.

"I told him that my family doesn't eat anything that would make them poop red. I gave him two options, he could move his garage, and after all he has an acre of land here, or, paint his roof white."

"I know what you mean; we have our problems at Boca Royale too!"

DEATH BY BLOGGING

Manasota Key FL (Storch Report) April 9, 2008 -- As you might imagine, I wasn't too happy Sunday reading a New York Times story with the headline, "In Web World of 24/7 Stress, Writers Blog Till They Drop."

All this time I thought I was enjoying myself, doing what I once did as a reporter – writing and meeting deadlines hoping that I would scoop the next reporter with an exclusive.

So I returned to what I loved, writing, but writing what I wanted to write, not covering a beat or every accident or murder that occurs on the street.

But there is a difference, I am working that 24/7 news cycle now and have been caught up in it for the past eight years. Now in between my days of reporting and my present hobby I was a Public Relations flack for the Pharmaceutical industry. Now, you want to talk about stress. But it's amazing how time goes by when you think you are having fun, only to pick up the Sunday paper to find out you have taken up a hobby that might be killing you?

Things have become so stressful after reading this Times' piece, that during the writing of this column, I reached for my Omron wrist blood pressure cuff and took my blood pressure, pulse and check for heart irregularities. My blood pressure was 106 over 61 with a pulse of 66 with no irregularities.

I'm always amazed at what these little gadgets can do.

However, after taking my blood pressure, which I consider a bit low, but they say that's good, I thought perhaps I should stop drinking my gin and tonic and have a coke, because the system seems to need some stimulation.

Now having done a bit of medical writing in my day I dug deeper into this article, for after all where was this headline coming from? You mean people were actually dying? Did they do a double blind study? Where's the credibility?

Well it didn't take me long to find out it was a study of three persons. Nevertheless, two of the three died. That's a high percentage, but I know you can't come up with a 'P' value to make this small sample statistically significant.

This report would never make the New England Journal of Medicine, I quickly thought.

So I checked the article further to find out that a couple of weeks ago they held a funeral service in North Lauderdale, Fla., – that's the State I blog from – who was a prolific blogger on technology and he died at the age of 60. Well, I got some comfort out of the fact that I've got 14 years on him.

Then there was another tech blogger who died of a massive coronary at the age of 50, well I got 24 years on him and as I mentioned the third blogger survived a heart attack and he was only 41, and I have 33 years on him.

Two of the three blogged on technology, well you're not going to see that subject in this column.

Now the author of this piece was very comforting when he said "to be sure, there is no official diagnosis of death by blogging, and the premature demise of two people obviously does not qualify as an epidemic."

But then they started talking to the living bloggers and the story really got bleak. One said, "I haven't died yet," and he was another one of those technology blogs. He said he has gained 30 pounds in the last three years, developed a severe sleeping disorder and turned his home into an office for him and four employees.

"At some point, I'll have a nervous breakdown and be admitted to the hospital or something else will happen," he said.

You know there are all kinds of bloggers out there, everyone wants to find a niche and something that scores financially like Google.

For those the stress is there, but there are many others of us that do it because it is fun. I always said no matter the job, the hobby, the sport or the exercise, if it's no longer fun stop doing it.

I wonder however, is my blood pressure too low?

EROTICISM SPIKES FINANCIAL RISK IN MEN

Manasota Key FL (Storch Report) April 5, 2008 -- I always wondered where men's sexual drive and financial acumen was located.

Now I know, as a result of a new study involving some 15 heterosexual young men at Stanford University.

I always thought it was a lot lower in the male anatomy, but it's actually located in the sex and money hub, the V-shaped nucleus accumbens, which sits near the base of the brain and plays a central role in what man experiences as pleasure, or in this case taking a risk with his money.

You see they did this study showing young men erotic pictures and when they saw them they were more likely to make a larger financial gamble than if they were shown a picture of something scary, such as a snake, or something neutral, such as a stapler.

I don't know who it is that comes up with these studies, but I want to tell you, I'm not going anywhere when I see an erotic picture, but when I see a snake I'm going to take off in my New Balance running shoes, or, look for a machete.

In either case I'm not going to take more risk with my money.

But apparently the arousing pictures in this study lit up the same part of the brain that lights up when financial risks are taken.

"You have a need in an evolutionary sense for both money and women. They trigger the same brain area," said Camelli Kuhnen, a Northwestern University finance professor who conducted the study with a Stanford University psychologist.

And all this time I thought it was Viagra that made these sexual and financial decisions for me?

They say in this study that when that hub, the nucleus accumbens, is activated by erotic images, the men were far more likely to bet high on a random chance game that would earn them either a dollar or a dime. Each man made more than 50 gambles under brain scans.

Now when I delved further into this study I found that it didn't matter if the sexy woman didn't tell me anything about the odds of winning a roulette game, what mattered is that the sexy woman is having an emotional impact. And this emotional impact bleeds over into my financial decisions.

So that is why I bought those high end sexually attractive cars while that erotic woman was standing alongside?

They say in the study there is something going on between the power of emotion and arousal and financial decisions.

Furthermore they say the link between sex and greed goes back hundreds of thousands of years, to men's evolutionary role as provider or resource gatherer to attract women.

Harvard economist Terry Burnham, author of the book, "Mean Genes." says this all makes sense. He says it's like the line from the movie "Scarface."

"In this country, you gotta make the money first. Then when you get the money, you get the power. Then when you get the power, then you get the women."

And so this study seems to come at a most appropriate time.

I now better understand former Governor Eliot Spitzer's actions with a hooker and his successor, David Paterson, admitting to multiple affairs. It seems to have something to do with the nucleus accumbens.

Now this same condition has affected presidents as well, after all it was not that long ago that President Bill Clinton risked all

with his affair with Monica Lewinsky. He left the White House $12 million in debt and seven years later he reported income of $109 million.

This study should be a wakeup call for Sen. Hillary Clinton, presidential candidate, for after all she, better than most knows of her husband's track record, and now with all that money in the Clinton's coffers she had best limit the number of erotic images that come before Bill, for after all she may not make it back into the White House.

I KNOW WHO WILL TAKE THAT 3 AM CALL, AND IT'S NOT CLINTON

Manasota Key Fl (Storch Report) April 2, 2008 --So I've been getting up at 3 AM to take a call and I fell asleep waiting for the ring.

One night I called the White House to see if they were awake and I got a White House Counselor in India.

I just don't get what this 3 AM thing is all about?

When I called the White House, I wasn't surprised that I got someone in India, for most of the time when I dial any number I get India.

There are Clinton ads about 3 AM, the first one was directed at Obama pointing out that he didn't have enough foreign policy experience to answer the phone at 3 AM, the second was about McCain who didn't answer the phone because he couldn't handle a discussion on the economy or the housing crisis.

I always wondered whether these important calls would come in on the red phone – and is the red phone in the President's ear while he or she sleeps or is doing something else in the bedroom?

I always envisioned Hillary in sexy lingerie cuddling Bill, whether it be when she was first lady or, highly unlikely, when she's on top as President.

And it crossed my mind, why 3 AM? Why not 2 AM or 4 AM?

Now if someone called my house at 3 AM it would be okay because we have a human day watch and a night watch and someone would always be up. I don't even know why we have an ADT security system.

That 3 AM call is really an important issue in this campaign according to the Clintons, because it's something like Jimmy Buffett's cocktail hour, 'it's always 5 PM somewhere.'

Someone said the only reason Hillary Clinton would answer the red phone at 3 AM would be to find out she lost another super delegate.

HILLARY'S ENTITLEMENT TALK WITH BILL

New York (Storch Report) March 25, 2008 -- "Good Morning Hillary. Good night's sleep?

"As a matter of fact Bill, I had a rather bad dream."

"What was that?"

"Oh, I didn't get the entitlement vote that I expected in this race for the presidential nomination, you know as the way in which we discussed it in college."

"I mean, I thought we set the country's perception for the fact that I was going to be the next president for 8 years?"

"Well, Hon, I thought that too, and I thought it was working well . . . that is until Obama got into the race."

"He's a rather slippery one . . . he can dance well, eat water melon at the same time and dodge bullets as well as you did in Bosnia."

"Bill, you know that was not very nice."

"Look Hillary, I tried. I pulled every race card I knew as well as one on patriotism in this campaign, and it didn't stick." What do you want me to do?"

"I told you to come out immediately with a statement on Rev. Jeremiah Wright, saying that 'he wouldn't have been your pastor.'"

"I'm going to use that one Bill, following my "misspoke" on the Bosnia issue."

"But, I always thought perception was reality?

"Yes, Hillary that is often the case. I think the key here is for you to get more popular votes then him, show the super delegates that you can beat McCain and the nomination will be yours."

"But, Bill that's an uphill battle, he has more democratic votes, more votes overall and he leads in delegate votes."

"Yes, but in the next set of primaries you must beat him in the popular vote, which will be our key to success."

"Then we can pull some of our dirty tricks and get the super delegates to swing our way. I think we need to take this to the floor of the convention."

"Let's face it Bill, your good friend Bill 'Judas' Richardson's betrayed us."

"The rats are jumping ship.

"I've been thinking Bill, with all the news about sex among our Governors and Mayors, do you think it would be appropriate for me to come out of the closet at this time? After all they are getting a lot of nice play. Perhaps it would give me the boost that I need?"

"I'm sure it will give you something along those lines Hillary, great idea. I'll call Matt Drudge."

A CALL FOR CELIBACY IN OUR NEXT PRESIDENT

Washington DC (Storch Report) March 19, 2008 -- From the White House to the Governor's houses across this land, from the Senate to the Congress there seems to be one consistent item on the agenda of our politicians – sex – and I for one, think we should request our next president be celibate.

I mean after all this has proven to be a major distraction from administration to administration whether it be on the State level, the congressional level or within that citizens' home of ours called the White House.

As if we haven't had enough with former New York Gov. Eliot Spitzer's trysts with hookers, now we have the new Governor of New York David Paterson and his wife, Michelle, admitting to multiple affairs with lovers and others, one of whom is currently working in the Governor's office.

Then there is the former New Jersey Gov. James McGreevy, who comes out of the closet, resigns and admits to a ménage a trios with his gay lover and his estranged wife.

And now the AP is reporting today that Hillary Rodham Clinton was in the White House on a half dozen days when her husband had sexual encounters with Monica Lewinsky.

This all came about because the media took a look at her calendar of the past, which was released today, and compared her schedule on days when Lewinsky said she had sexual encounters with President Bill Clinton.

My god what happened to that good common sense cliché, "when the cats away the mice will play." Bill didn't wait until the cat was away he played right under Hillary's nose a half-a-dozen times when she was in the White House. Now there's an astute presidential candidate! Imagine an intelligence program under Hillary's administration?

Now if you don't think sex is a major distraction when one has to deal with wars, the economy, jobs, foreign policy, healthcare, greeting heads of state, holding parties, keeping peace with congress and then working in your sexual activities you have another thought coming.

But imagine trying to schedule sexual events when your wife is in the White House and to do this over a three year period — that's not only chutzpah, but requires a social secretary with special talent.

I can just hear the words coming from outside the oval office, "Bill what are you doing in there?"

"Oh, Hillary, I'm just working on the State of the Union."

I mean after all, what would be wrong with asking our political candidates to commit to celibacy?

What would be wrong with having presidential debates on sexual activities past, present and future intentions?

After all I could see where we might hold a Summit in the Vatican, hosted by the Pope, where discussions could take place for the recruitment of politicians who would commit to celibacy while holding office.

We might consider recruiting these leaders from Monasteries and Convents.

Oh, I know what you are going to say about this idea, the Vatican and its Priests too have had their sexual scandals, and I am sure the

Convents are not void of them either. But the boys and girls have been quite as of late and maybe they cleaned up their act?

Now I realize that for every good idea you should have a check and balance.

What I would suggest here is that we have someone like Lorena Bobbitt to serve as the equivalent of first lady or first man – then there would be no more naiveté or distractions to our politician's duties.

WHO YA GONNA VOTE FOR HERBIE?

Miami Beach FL (Storch Report) March 15, 2008 -- On a park bench in South Beach: "Hey Herbie, how are you?" "Oh, I'm fine Moshe, how are you?" "Well I've been thinking of all the times we've been meeting like this here, we have seen this place come and go and come and go and it's back again." "Yeh, so what?

"Well, Herbie, I was wondering who you are going to vote for?" "Moshe, what the hell does who I'm going to vote for got to do with this place coming and going?"

"Herbie, haven't you been reading the papers how Florida could play a big role in who the democratic nominee might be, and we could have another chance to vote again?"

"Moshe, what difference does it make, it didn't count the first time, what makes you think it will count the second time?

"Herbie, who is running?"

"Oh, I'm not sure, but I think it's between that white woman who is married to a former president who found Monica in the oval office and that black man who found Jesus from his pastor-friend in Chicago."

"What difference does it make Moshe; it's the same old same old. We've been talking about this since we were kids in the Bronx. Nothing changes."

"Oh, no Herbie this year is different they're talking about 'change.'"

"What's the change?

"Well this year we could be voting for a white woman president or a black man president. We've never had either one of those before and having two at the same time would be a double treat.

"And, as I understand it, the contest is so close they both could be on the same ticket.

"And, Herbie this would be just like us going to the Fontainebleau for an expensive ice cream soda."

"Now how is that Moshe?"

"Well, we could have our favorite, a black and white, or a white and black ice cream soda, and as for change they say they are both interchangeable, although as for the status quo – they would still be expensive.

"Moshe, I think you better put your hat on, your forehead is getting a bit red."

FLORIDA AN ELECTION LIGHTING ROD?

Miami FL (Storch Report) March 6, 2008 -- Florida gets more than its share of lighting hits annually and doesn't really need anymore, but the Democratic Party seems to select this state for unwarranted election year lightning bolts that seem to play a role in the selection of our next president.

Florida doesn't ask to be the focal point, but when it is selected to be such, history shows it can step up to the plate.

Is history repeating itself?

Why should party rules override the Constitution?

Why are we the people not selecting who should be President and Vice President of the United States?

Why is the democratic process being manipulated by party politics?

The Democrats created a problem in Florida and Michigan. By telling each state they could not hold their primaries before the first party sanctioned date in February, and if they did there would be penalties.

Florida and Michigan defied these party rules and little did the Democrats realize in penalizing these states by not recognizing the delegates nor allowing them to attend the convention, that they would not have selected a Presidential nominee at this point in time, and as a result, Florida and Michigan could be the states that selects the Democratic nominee . . . or perhaps implodes the party.

So the Democrats have a dilemma facing them that they did not anticipate.

The solution is not simple.

Primaries were held in both states. Obama wasn't on the ballot in Michigan, Clinton was. Neither campaigned in either state.

The only solution is to hold second primaries in both states. But who's going to pay for the primaries – certainly not I as a resident of Florida.

If the primaries already held in both states are upheld, the popular vote between Clinton and Obama would be a difference of 3,000 votes in favor of Obama.

I for one believe that the Democrats created the problem; therefore it is theirs' to resolve and pay for should there be a need for a second primary in Florida.

However, I do have one constructive suggestion: Katherine Harris, former Secretary of State in the year 2,000, and a two term Republican Congresswoman is still living in this state and I believe that she could solve this crisis, for she knows how to deal with hanging and pregnant chads.

MY BABY, MADE IN INDIA

Bombay, India (Storch Report) March 4, 2008 -- I'm thinking of having a child, and having it labeled, "Made in India.

I don't know if you heard about it, but reproductive outsourcing is a rapidly expanding enterprise in India.

We are all used to buying a cell phone, a computer or for that matter any electronic device and when we have a problem with it we call an 800 number and talk to India.

It doesn't matter where the product was made or bought; the solution to any issue with the electronic device is in India.

So I thought I would get a baby from India.

And why not, all other forms of outsourcing are already there, in fact the outsourcing business is so big they already have to pay more for their current skilled workers, that India is outsourcing its outsourcing to developing countries before their clients do so, so they don't lose the base of their current outsourcing business.

Reproductive outsourcing is new in India and rapidly expanding. Commercial surrogacy was legalized in India in 2002.

I really don't want another child, but it seems as though I can pick one up for about $25,000 and that includes the cost of the medical procedure, air tickets and hotels for two trips to India, one for the fertilization and a second to collect the baby.

There are plenty of reasons to get a baby from India, rather than a Madras jacket. First of all Indian women are for the most

part free of vices, like alcohol smoking and drugs. Secondly, I can pick the profile of my egg donor, you know like one with a high education level.

I don't have to worry about the mother trying to claim the baby because they sign away all their rights to the child. The surrogate mother provides a womb for an embryo formed from the sperm and egg of the parent or parents. It is only the name of the genetic parents that appear on the birth certificate.

It seems to me that it could be quite a good investment, for I can amortize the cost over a five to 10 year period and dozens of electronic devices. By then the child will be old enough to answer and solve all the questions I might have for my cell phone, computer, TV set, car, cameras, surround sound, and i-pods and I will never have to talk to India again.

WHY DOES THE NAME OBAMA COME UP OSAMA WHEN I DO A SPELLCHECK ON MY COMPUTER?

Washington DC (Storch Report) February 28, 2008 --Names as of late seem to be creating political headlines with our candidates for President more than the substance of such issues as the Iraqi War, the economy, housing, healthcare and global warming during this chilly winter.

Now, I for one don't get it.

It seems to me that every time I write a column and mention the name Obama and then do a spellcheck on my writing, it suggests that Obama should be spelled Osama.

Now to be fair and balanced, I am working in Microsoft Vista. Check it out it, Obama comes out Osama every time on Microsoft spellcheck programs whether it's Vista or some earlier program, and there are no other spelling options.

So I went to my Apple laptop, which runs the Macintosh program. I typed in the name Obama and it didn't correct it to Osama with one choice, it gave me three choices – Ocala, Omaha, or Osaka.

Well, I thought that's a little bit better, none of those places are in the Middle East, but then again there are more Microsoft users than Mac users. I realized it wasn't much spelling help, but

then again if I wanted to raise race horses, buy steaks or visit the Orient, these were good leads.

Now I thought there must be some right wing conspiracy going on here, you know with all those right wing radio talk show hosts throwing these Middle Eastern names around casting innuendoes by word associations to famous evil people and casting aspersions on the leading Democratic candidate Barack Hussein Obama.

I didn't know his middle name was Hussein until Bill Cunningham; a popular conservative radio talk show host from Cincinnati, Ohio did a warm-up piece for a staged McCain rally.

Could it be that Obama was trying to play down his middle name for the same reasons the right wing might want to play it up?

Before McCain appeared, the radio host told the crowd he'd had a dream about "Barack Hussein Obama's wonderful life a year from today." In the dream, he said, "Obama was president and had just met with Iranian leader Mahmoud Ahmadinejad and was set to meet with North Korean leader Kim Jong II." Then Cunningham said, Obama was going to "saddle up next to Hezbollah."

"All's going to be right with the world when the great prophet from Chicago takes the stand, and the world leaders who want to kill us will simply be singing (Kumbaya) together around the table with Barack Obama," Cunningham said.

Well McCain went ballistic when he heard what Cunningham said, repudiated every word, apologized for the remarks, took full responsibility and said it would never happen again.

Asked whether Obama's middle name was an appropriate topic for discussion, McCain said, "No, it is not."

I wonder if he knows Obama's name comes up Osama on Microsoft spellcheck.

I find this middle name thing really interesting. Past presidents didn't seem to have a problem with their middle names. There was Franklin Delano Roosevelt, John Fitzgerald Kennedy, Richard Millhouse Nixon and William Jefferson Clinton.

In fact before John Fitzgerald Kennedy ever became president there was a lot of debate about the first Irish American Catholic running for president, but I don't remember any talk of Kennedy not using his middle name, or for that matter, trying to down play it.

So with this entire hullabaloo over names I thought it would be productive in this democracy to look into these names a bit further so the voters can deal with all the facts – to hell with the issues.

The meaning of Barack is 'blessed.' That seems to be a non-controversial start. The origin is African and it's from the Hebrew name Baruch and also has the meaning of 'good looking.' This kid is off to a good start.

But then it goes downhill, or uphill, depending upon your perspective. Now the name Hussein is Arabic and there is no question of its origin: Muslim, Iraqi, Iranian, and Pakistani.

Obama apparently gives the computer problems; perhaps that is why it comes out Osama. Modern vernacular says, 'chosen by voters.' It further states it's a Luo name male from Western Kenya, which may derive from 'obam' which connotes 'bending or leaning.'

Now if we look into Osama which the computer substitutes for Obama we find that its origin is Arabic and it means feline predator –'Lion-like.'

It is a form of Usama and nickname for the 'Lion.'

Now again, to be fair and balanced, I thought it only just that if I dissect Barack Hussein Obama's name, I should do the same to mine.

My full name is Donald John Storch, I go by Don Storch, but for no other reason other than to make it simple. All official papers are signed Donald John Storch and my college degree reads as such.

Now Donald – it's of Scottish and Gaelic origin. It means 'great chief, world mighty.'

John, it is of Hebrew origin, meaning 'Lord is gracious' and is biblical. There are two characters in the New Testament named John.

Storch, is obviously a descendent of the Stork – a bird. It is German, Middle High German.

After making a comparison with Obama, I'm thinking of running for president – I like my middle name.

IF YOU DON'T FIT IN THE SEAT YOU CAN'T EAT

Mississippi (Storch Report) February 3, 2008 -- I have an idea for the State of Mississippi where they just introduced a bill that would make it illegal for restaurants to serve the obese.

You know those luggage measuring devices they have in airline terminals just before you board the plane, if your carry-on bag doesn't fit within the device you must check it?

Well to help restaurant owners comply with the proposed law should it pass, they should include a provision where restaurants would be compelled to buy new and smaller seats, with the motto, If you don't fit in the seat you can't eat — it's the law.

Bill 282 was introduced this week and it would make it illegal for state-licensed restaurants to serve obese patrons.

The bill is the brainchild of three members of the state's House of Representatives, Republicans W.T. Mayhall, Jr. and John Read, and Democrat Bobby Shows.

The bill proposes that the state's Department of Health establish weight criteria after consultation with Mississippi's Council on Obesity.

However, the bill does not detail what penalties an eatery would face if its food was served to someone with an excessive body mass index.

You see with my seat compliance idea, it would be unnecessary to worry about the body mass index – if he/she didn't fit in the seat, no grub.

As it stands now a food establishment would be entitled to rely on the criteria for obesity in those written materials when determining whether or not it is allowed to serve food to any person.

And it would be up to the State Department of Health to monitor the food establishments for compliance, and they may revoke the permit of any food establishment that repeatedly violates the law.

With my seat compliance idea, enforcement would be easy for both the food establishment and the Department of Health. However, I would suggest the sponsors add an addendum to the bill that would allow the food establishment "chair charges" to any patron who tries to sit in the chair and can't get out.

ANOTHER BREAKFAST WITH HILLARY & BILL

New York NY (Storch Report) January 31, 2008 -- "Bill, we need to talk."

"Yes, Hillary what's on your mind?"

"Well, I'm wondering whether or not we should take you off the trail?"

"Off the trail Hillary? What do you think I am, Hopalong Cassidy? We talked about my role in your campaign, I delivered the messages based upon your campaign strategy."

"Are you saying the strategy has now changed?"

"Well, some of your messages have backfired and our experts are re-thinking the strategy to raise the race issue."

"Then you better let me know what the new strategy happens to be.

"Would you pass me the eggs benedict?"

"Be careful with them Bill, just take one."

"Don't tell me what to do Hillary, I'm the President, you're just a Senator."

"Bill don't pull rank on me, I've got some problems and I need your help."

"All right, what's your problem and how can I help?"

"Well it all began with your 'fairy tale' comments about Obama and then comparing his win in South Carolina with that of 'Jessie

Jackson's.' This clearly raised the race card issue. And I don't know if that was very wise — in retrospect.

"It backfired according to our strategists, and as a matter of fact with our supporters.

"And, your recent comments about the economy being good for global warming seemed to be ill-timed.

"And last night ABC served up some tough questions. Oh Bill, could you pass me another egg benedict — they are really very good.

"Oh, ABC . . . they actually asked me if I could control you and I said, 'of course.' And, as I know this is not true.

"Then they asked me if this was a co-presidency and I said no, the voters need to know who they are voting for," I said.

"Well Hillary that was certainly a non sequitur, I think we need to stay the course — you have the most delegates and that's what counts.

"You know this is a co-presidency, that's the way we planned it in law school. I just never thought we would be up against a black, that's why it's important to play the race card.

"Let's stay the course and as we discussed and rehearsed, throw in a tear or two; that always gets to the voters, especially when a woman let's it roll down her cheek."

"Okay Bill."

A TWO-HEADED PRESIDENCY?

Onboard Air Hillary (Storch Report) January 22, 2008 -- Hillary and Bill are onboard her private jet on their way to South Carolina and the next primary, both getting their taste buds adjusted to eating hominy grits for breakfast.

"Gees. Bill these grits are terrible."

"Get used to them there are a few votes in them there grits."

"I know Bill, I really never knew what you went through to get in the White House."

"Hillary, you don't want to know!"

"But it seems our strategy is working, you know, drawing Obama into a pissing contest with a skunk?"

"Hill, I told you that from the get-go. It was a mistake to let him take the high road. We now have him where we want him wrestling him in the pig pen.

"No one wants to wrestle a pig in the mud, because the pig loves it."

"You were absolutely right Bill. Do you think the American public will really go for a two-headed presidency?"

"Well, let's not immediately jump to that conclusion."

"You know, Bill they are already speculating about that."

"Listen, Hillary the public is much today as Barnum and Bailey said they were yesterday, "there's a sucker born every day."

"Follow my lead, we have a one two punch going."

"You're a shoo-in."

"Well, I hope so Bill, this is the way we planned it in law school."

Fast forward: Hillary and Bill get the Democratic nomination for President and lose to John McCain in a landslide.

The exit polls showed that the voters would rather have two Siamese elephants attached at the trunks, to run this country, than a two-headed Clinton presidency.

HOW TO MAKE AN ANDROID HUMAN

Iowa (Storch Report) January 10, 2008 -- Inside the Hillary Clinton War Room, following her poor showing in Iowa, the brain trusts were scrambling for ideas to make her the 'comeback kid.'

They knew they had to come up with something, or the Clintons were going to bring in Democratic strategists James Carville and Paul Begala, sooner than later, but they didn't want it to happen now at the expense of their jobs.

They knew that Bill had already publicly called Hillary the 'comeback kid' after her poor showing in Iowa and that this was their signal to produce or else.

They were ready to move on to the next primary, but were still in Iowa.

The polls were predicting a win for Barack Obama by 9 points in New Hampshire.

They had to come up with the 'big idea'.

Then it dawned on one of those bright young faces with pimples still overflowing from puberty, "How about the coffee shop media idea?"

Everyone in the room looked somewhat puzzled, and someone said, "The coffee shop media idea?"

"You know that's the one we discussed where we stage a media event in a coffee shop, a controlled environment, with a select group of Democrats that are friendly to Hillary and we have a one

on one conversation where she finally answers some questions, but planted ones, that she is prepared to answer."

"Okay", another war room participant said, "Where does that take us?"

"Well, if you remember this is where we play the crying card."

"During our media training sessions we had her go through a few staged interviews where she evoked tears during the interview . . . you know, in order to make her appear human."

"After all, let's face it we are dealing with an Android candidate and we have to put a human face on her."

"You better be careful, the walls may have ears."

"Well I'm just calling a spade a shovel, and we're between a rock and a hard place right now."

"Who's our plant?"

"Well, she's a friend of one of our campaign workers and the best part of it she brings credibility to the table, because she has already declared that she is voting for Obama, but admires and respects Hillary."

"What is her question?"

"She will just ask Hillary how she was holding up to the rigors of the race, and it will be the last question.

"This will be Hillary's cue to deliver an emotional answer and to be on the verge of tears while doing so."

"It very well could be the tipping-tear point of the campaign."

"You think it will work?"

"You mean we could tear-drop our way into the White House?"

"You bet, Americans love to root for the underdog, especially when she's a woman showing emotion."

The plan was executed with the approval of the Android.

EPILOGUE: HOW THESE WRITINGS CAME ABOUT

I was having dinner with a writer friend, Larry Galton and his wife, at the Royal Hawaiian on the beach of Waikiki in the early 70's when the conversation drifted toward the philosophical.

We were debriefing in Hawaii after a crisis management assignment in Japan.

Larry, a renowned author of medical books, asked if there was anyone along the way in my career at that time that had an impact on my life. Without hesitation I said Gorham Munson, a creative writing professor I had in college.

Larry and his wife looked at each other and then me in astonishment.

It was then that Larry revealed that he and Gorham began their writing careers together in a loft they shared in Greenwich Village, N.Y. Larry's wife was a literary agent.

I had known both Gorham and Larry for the same previous decade and we would see each other frequently, but separately, not knowing we each had a mutual friend in common during the same period, until that night at the Royal Hawaiian. But by then Gorham had died.

I first met Gorham Munson at a creative writing class at Fairleigh Dickinson University, on the Madison N.J. campus.

He walked into the classroom wearing a black suit, white shirt and black tie. He removed a black homburg hat revealing a shock of white hair and then rested his cane on the desk.

I can still hear the first words he uttered to the class, "You are not a writer until you have written a million words."

He had revealed a bit about himself at the time, but nowhere near the amount I was about to find out later, and unfortunately much too late.

He was one of the early instructors at the famous Bread Loaf Writer's Conference at Middlebury College, where he studied, he wrote Robert Frost's biography and launched the creative writing program at the New School in N.Y in 1931.

I took to Gorham's creative writing class like a duck takes to water. He apparently liked my writing style and our personalities seem to click. I got an A in the class and Gorham continued to stay in touch with me, I always wished I put out the same effort he did..

After I graduated from college I took a public relations job with a pharmaceutical company preceded by a four year stint as a reporter and editor for a local daily newspaper.

He continued to send me postcards from his different travels around the world and we would frequently have dinner at Rod's Ranch House in Convent Station NJ, after which he would teach an evening class in creative writing at Fairleigh.

Then one day I received a call from him at work asking me if I could get some time off to be a substitute instructor, he said kind of like "John the Baptist" for a well-known writer that could only make one week of the two weeks writer's conference he was conducting at Fairleigh Dickinson University.

I jumped at the opportunity, that is, with the approval of my boss who was more than supportive.

I would give three lectures in nonfiction writing during the first week and review and critique the student's writings.

It was a heady environment and was well worth the time and effort I put into it. The mere thought that Gorham selected me to pinch-hit for a literary giant, overcame the token $100 check I received from the University for my services.

Along with the remuneration, I could also offer someone a two week scholarship to the writer's conference. I picked an editor of a weekly newspaper who was interested in writing fiction.

Among the instructor's at the writer's conference was Sloan Wilson, author of "The Man in the Gray Flannel Suit" and "A Summer Place", both books were made into movies.

Gorham was the classic mentor, but little did I know at the time, that he had been a mentor to some of the great names in literary history.

To this day I am humbled by him seeking me out to the degree he did and I feel rather stupid, with innate reporter skills at the time, for not pursuing his friendship and professional relationship more than I did at the time.

Then one day as I was going through my daily read at work of the New York Times and I came upon Gorham's obituary.

It ran two columns in width and the length of the page. And, what I didn't know about my friend and mentor was truly astounding.

Between 1929 and 1941, Gorham served on the faculty of the prestigious Bread Loaf Writers' Conference nine times.

The impulse to establish the "Conference on Writing" came initially from Robert Frost, who loved the inspiring setting of Middlebury. Frost appeared at Bread Loaf a record 25 times since its inception. In 2005 it marked its 80th conference.

Among the writers, authors and editors attracted to Bread Loaf over the years were Stephen Vincent Benet, Robert Frost, Sinclair Lewis, Gorham Munson, Archibald MacLeish and John Ciardi.

In 1931, as posted by The New School, "distinguished editor Gorham Munson offered the first writing workshop," and he was so honored by the school with a citation for his leadership and foresight.

Today the New School offers a graduate writing program leading to the MFA degree with concentrations in Fiction, Poetry, Nonfiction and Writing for Children.

If you do a search on the Internet today for Gorham Munson, you will come up with more than 14,000 mentions.

Hart Crane, the poet (1899-1932) had an original audience that included editors and readers of the little magazines of the 1920's fellow poets, and literary friends such as Malcolm Cowley, Harry and Caresse Crosby, Waldo Frank, Gorham Munson, Katherine Anne Porter, and Allen Tate.

Hart Crane sought-out Gorham as a mentor. But he wasn't the only one, as the stories on the Internet confirm. One writer traveled to Paris to visit with him only to find that Munson had returned to New York, and his apartment was occupied by Ernest Hemingway.

Among the books available by Gorham Munson are" Robert Frost, Making Poems for America; 12 Decisive Battles of the Mind: the Story of Propaganda During the Christian era; Germany between Two Wars: A Study of Propaganda; Robert Frost: A Study in Sensibility & Good Sense; Waldo Frank; Destinations; Style and Forms In American Prose; and The Dilemma of the Liberated. I recently ordered the following Munson books, The Awakening Twenties: A Memoir-History of a Literary Period; and the Written Word: How to Write for Readers.

In 1985 The Awakening Twenties was published, a book Gorham finished before he died and his widow Elizabeth Delza Munson, who I met at the Writer's Conference Gorham asked me to be 'John the Baptist', was responsible for having it published.

A New York Times review by Christopher Lehmann-Haupt noted that there was a key word in the title, "Awakening" and he said about that, "We think the era as roaring and jazzy, but Gorham Munson digs beneath the clichés to a more complex reality. America, he believes, was awakening from its provincialism – in the sense of both its rural way of life and its unawareness of European culture. At the same time, America was awakening to its own possibilities as a culture, a result no doubt of the perspective that the new awareness of Europe provided. Finally, America was awakening from its narrow Puritanism – which

may sound like the greatest cliché of all, but apparently you had to be there to appreciate just how oppressive that Puritanism really was.

"Gorham was there and he puts the reader there in these reflective interlocking essays."

Gorham Munson was a mentor to writers but a writer, editor and author himself; but more importantly to me, a teacher and friend.

ACKNOWLEDGEMENT

I would like to express my appreciation to the late Gorham Munson, a mentor and friend, who said you're not a writer until you've written a million words; to the late Dick Holub, PhD., Professor of English at Fairleigh Dickinson University, who taught me to be astutely observant; and to Norman B. Tomlinson Jr., former Publisher of Morris County's Daily Record, who hired me as a reporter and told me to write it as though I was talking to my Mother.

I would also like to thank Michael White, illustrator, from Sarasota, Florida, for capturing in his cover illustration the essence of the writings in this book and for making my caricature on the author's page to appear more pleasant than I am.

ABOUT THE AUTHOR

Don Storch was a journalist, editor, corporate public relations executive, and crisis and issue management consultant.

He currently is a conservative columnist and author writing for the website DonStorch.com, home of the Storch Report. Don's columns rank in the first percentile of the Blogtoplist of political columnists and is read in more than 50 countries.

He is a graduate of Fairleigh Dickinson University.

He and his wife live on Manasota Key, a barrier reef on the Southwest Coast of Florida.

www.ingramcontent.com/pod-product-compliance
Lightning Source LLC
Chambersburg PA
CBHW070103290526
45789CB00005B/1908

* 9 7 8 1 5 0 0 9 5 5 6 3 2 *